CYNTHIA UNGER

Lovin Nature through awareness and reflection.

A journey of self love and the magic that unfolds.

This book was professionally typeset on Reedsy.
Find out more at reedsy.com

The life I touch for good or ill will touch another life, and in turn another, until who knows where the trembling stops or in what far place my touch will be felt.

Frederick Buechner

Contents

Preface

This book comes from profound gratitude for the beautiful life I have built from the lessons I've gathered through life's challenges and triumphs, shaped by the people, places, and ideas that have left an indelible mark on me.

It is an invitation to slow down, reflect, and embrace the beauty of life's interconnections—a journey of self-discovery that begins with awareness and grows through kindness and connection. I believe that every action, thought, and intention carries a ripple that extends far beyond what we can see. This belief has guided me to live more intentionally and to explore the profound ways we can guide our lives and impact one another.

Through these pages, I hope to inspire you to reflect on your own journey, to find joy in the little things, and to embrace the magic that comes from self-love and compassion. My wish is that you feel empowered to write your own story, one filled with light, growth, and endless possibilities. Stay curious, stay open and continue to seek understanding.

Thank you for joining me on this journey. Together, let's create ripples of kindness and gratitude that reach far and wide.

Acknowledgments

This book is the culmination of a journey inspired by many extraordinary individuals, both deeply personal and widely influential.

To Napoleon Hill, Wayne Dyer, Bob Proctor, Abraham Hicks, and Rhonda Byrne—your teachings have illuminated my path, shaping my understanding of Universal Laws and revealing the profound connection between thought, energy, and action. Your wisdom has been a constant source of inspiration, encouraging me to explore, grow, and align with the life I've imagined.

To my family, my foundation of love and strength—your unwavering support has given me the courage to dream. To my husband, my steadfast partner, and my children, who inspire me every day to be my best self—you are the heart of everything I do. To my siblings, my lifelong teammates, for showing me encouragement, the power of resilience and shared history.

To LuAnn, your kindness and example have been a guiding light, showing me what's possible. To Shelly, your wisdom and encouragement have been an anchor, keeping me grounded while listening to my ever evolving dreams.

To my colleagues and coworkers—thank you for the lessons learned in persistence, collaboration, and adaptability. The insights gained through working alongside you have shaped my understanding of teamwork, growth, and inspired action.

Finally, to all those who've walked this journey with me, offering words of encouragement, moments of insight, or simply setting an example to follow, I am deeply grateful. This book is a tapestry woven from gratitude, kindness, and connection.

Thank you for believing in me and for being part of this incredible journey.

1

Chapter 1

The Seed of Transformation

There's a moment in everyone's life when you can feel the shift—a subtle but powerful stirring that signals something greater is about to unfold. For me, it wasn't a lightning-bolt revelation, but a quiet awareness, like a seed taking root in fertile soil. It was the beginning of a journey that would redefine how I saw myself, my health, and the world around me.

Looking back, I realize it wasn't just one event that sparked this transformation, but a series of small, seemingly unrelated decisions that eventually blossomed into something far more profound. Each choice was like a brushstroke on the canvas of my life—a gentle, deliberate mark that, with time, painted the picture of a life well-lived, aligned with nature, health, and self-love.

This book is about those moments—the quiet shifts, the daily rituals, the small acts of self-compassion that, over time, can turn an ordinary life into something magical. It's about finding power in simplicity, knowing that the tiniest actions, when done with intention, can ripple out and create something extraordinary.

I didn't arrive here overnight. My life—just like yours—has been a steady process of growth, discovery, and refinement. Along the way, I've picked up practices, ideas, and perspectives that have enriched my journey. Some I learned from books, others from mentors, friends, and family members, and still more from the quiet whispers of nature itself.

But above all, I've learned to trust myself—to trust that the journey, no matter how slow or winding, is always moving me toward a better version of who I'm meant to be.

And here, in this book, I'm sharing those lessons with you. Not as a road map to follow step-by-step, but as a collection of seeds—ideas and practices you can plant in your own life when the timing feels right. Together, we'll explore the beauty of self-care rituals, the magic of nature, and the incredible power of self-compassion. I'll show you how small, intentional changes can unlock something magnificent inside you, just as they did for me.

So, are you ready to take that first step with me? Let's plant the seed together and watch the magic unfold.

For me, that first step began with a very practical goal: to transform my body after pregnancy. As a young mother, I wanted to build the energy needed to keep up with a young child while balancing the responsibilities of a growing family and a demanding job. Taking off those extra pounds wasn't easy, even though I'd gone into motherhood young and thin. But I realized that walking was an exercise I could fit into my life consistently, no matter how busy things got.

At first, walking was purely functional. It was something I could do with my child, during my lunch breaks at work, or even by intentionally parking further from my destination. Those small adjustments added up, creating a rhythm in my day that gave me a sense of control over my health. Slowly but surely, I noticed changes—not just in my body, but in my energy levels, mood and patience.

What started as a way to reclaim my physical fitness became something more. Walking brought me clarity, balance, and moments of peace in an otherwise chaotic life. It was during these walks that I realized how much I needed this time for myself—not just to move, but to breathe, to think, and to reset. It became my foundation, a simple yet powerful tool that proved how small, consistent actions could create meaningful change.

As the seed of transformation began to grow, I found myself drawn to other practices that, like walking, seemed simple but carried profound wisdom. These weren't grand gestures or sweeping changes, but small rituals—acts of care that helped me slow down, reflect, and connect with my deeper self. Walking was just the start, the first tool in my growing toolbox, and it laid the groundwork for all that was to come.

One of the first rituals I embraced was as simple as stepping outside. Whether it was in the early morning light or under a canopy of stars, nature became my sanctuary. It didn't matter if I was barefoot in the grass, walking along the shoreline, or simply sitting in the backyard—there was a kind of magic in those moments. Nature has a way of grounding us, reminding us of the beauty and balance that exists beyond the noise of daily life.

As I spent more time outdoors, my love for nature grew deeper. It became more than just a peaceful escape; it turned into a necessary act of self-love and discovery. Nature taught me to slow down, to listen—not just to the wind or the rustling leaves, but to myself. The more time I spent outdoors, the more I realized how much nature could teach me about resilience, patience, and growth.

One favorite place to visit was the beach. Living within biking distance made it a frequent destination, and it wasn't long before biking itself became a cherished activity. It never felt like exercise; it was always an adventure. Exploring on a bike brought a sense of freedom, and to this day, our bicycles are a constant companion on vacations. They're not just a mode of travel—they're a gateway to fun and exploration.

It was at the beach that I first connected with the practice of grounding—barefoot in the sand, feeling the earth beneath me. That simple act became a ritual of its own, and it extended into other areas of my life. Walking barefoot in the grass, feeling the cool, soft blades underfoot, brought a kind of peace that was both physical and emotional. It's amazing how something so simple can feel so deeply restorative.

Yoga entered my life soon after. Strength training had already become part of my routine—a way to build a strong body and a strong mind. But yoga introduced me to balance and flexibility, not just in my body but in my approach to life. Meditation followed yoga, and together they created a space for me to connect with myself on a deeper level. And through it all, walking remained a steady companion. It was where it all began, and I've never let it fall away.

Not every form of exercise has come as naturally. I've tried jogging and may try again, but it hasn't quite fit into my life yet. Strength training, on the other hand, has become a tool I return to when life calls for resilience. I've learned that exercise, when approached with intention, becomes more than physical movement—it becomes a reflection of what I need most in the moment. Yoga for balance, grounding for clarity, strength training for resolve—they've all found their place in my life, ebbing and flowing as life calls for action.

Through these practices, I've discovered that living intentionally isn't about rigid routines but about listening to what my body and spirit need. The journey is ever-evolving, and each step brings me closer to living in harmony with myself and the world around me.

Another simple ritual that became foundational was making my bed each morning. At first, it seemed trivial—a chore I'd often overlooked. But soon, I realized it was much more than that. Making the bed wasn't just about tidying up; it was about setting the tone for my day. It was an act of completion, a small victory to start the morning with purpose and clarity. In those few moments, I claimed control over my environment and created a sense of order, no matter what chaos might follow. It became a reminder that even the smallest actions have the power to shape our mindset.

These seemingly mundane acts began to build on one another, creating a framework of self-care that supported my personal growth. What I discovered was this: it's not the complexity of the rituals that matters, but the consistency with which we practice them. Each time we honor our bodies, our minds, and our environment, we nurture the seed of transformation. Over time, these small actions cultivate a life rooted in intention and mindfulness.

One of my favorite rituals involves water—specifically, the long baths I take with a blend of Epsom salt, cinnamon, coconut oil, and other natural ingredients. What started as a simple way to unwind became something much deeper. These baths are more than a physical cleanse; they've become sacred moments of reflection and renewal. Each ingredient carries its own energy: salt for grounding, cinnamon for warmth and circulation, coconut oil for nourishment. Together, they transform the bath into a healing space where I can let go of stress and realign with my intentions.

It's in these quiet moments that I'm reminded of the larger philosophy I've embraced: self-care isn't selfish—it's essential. It's not about indulgence or luxury; it's about honoring the relationship you have with yourself. These rituals, approached with intention, become acts of love—not just for the body, but for the soul.

As I sit down to share this journey with you, I can already feel the trans-formative power that comes with putting my thoughts into words. Writing this book has been one of the most empowering experiences of my life. It's helped me reflect on where I've been, where I'm going, and how much I've grown along the way.

I encourage you to consider doing the same—not necessarily writing a book, but finding a way to capture your journey. Whether through journaling, storytelling, or simply sitting quietly with your thoughts, you'll find that reflection can be a powerful tool for growth. By looking back, you'll see how far you've come and discover new ways to nurture the seeds of transformation in your own life.

There's something magical that happens when we take the time to reflect on our own stories, our own rituals, and our own growth.

By the time we reach the end of this book, I believe you'll feel that same empowerment—the kind that gives you the courage to take a step forward, perhaps even to start writing your own story. You don't have to follow my exact path, but I believe you'll find inspiration to create a journey of your own that leads to great success, joy, and a life lived in alignment with your deepest values.

Breaking through

I've come to realize that many of us carry a quiet belief that we're not good enough or somehow undeserving of greatness. It's a common thread in human experience, and I've lived it too. But once you break through that barrier, there's a world on the other side—one filled with possibility. I've been there, and it feels lighter, more open. Others around me have been there too, and like so many others, we sometimes slip back.

I remind myself often: the journey is full of lessons, and that's where the magic lies. Learning is empowering. Every time we face our feelings—whether it's fear, jealousy, grief, or guilt—we grow. These emotions are part of us. They shouldn't be shoved aside or ignored. Instead, they deserve to be acknowledged and understood. Sometimes, yes, we need to set them down gently, letting them wait for a more appropriate time, when we're ready to face them fully. But we must come back to them, allowing space to feel and to heal.

Heavy emotions can be exhausting to carry. But eventually, we learn to set them down, to look at them with fresh eyes and ask ourselves: *What can I control? What can I do next?* And sometimes, the best plan is simply to rest. Taking a nap, stepping away, or giving yourself permission to pause is not giving up—it's an act of self-care and a powerful strategy for renewal.

The Power of Self-Compassion

Self-compassion is the thread that weaves through all of this. It's what allows us to carry on, to keep learning, and to grow from the weight of what we've experienced. When we give ourselves grace, we find the strength to move forward, even in the face of life's hardest challenges.

You'll discover that the quicker you return to self-compassion, the quicker you'll find peace on the other side of those heavy moments. And when you do, you'll realize something profound: you are capable, worthy, and deserving of greatness.

So let's plant the seed, nurture it with care, and let the magic unfold. Together, we'll embrace the journey, not as a destination, but as an ever-evolving process of growth, healing, and becoming.

What small ritual could you incorporate into your life today to plant the seed of transformation?

These small, intentional acts opened my eyes to a universal truth: the forces that shape our lives often work in harmony with the laws of nature and the universe itself. Exploring these laws would deepen my journey in unexpected ways.

2

Chapter 2

Aligning with the 12 Universal Laws of Nature

As I delved deeper into my journey, I began to realize that the rituals I was practicing were more than just isolated actions. They were tools—pieces of a larger framework that connected me to something greater. Each act, from walking to grounding to mindful reflection, fit together like puzzle pieces, forming what I began to call my "toolbox for transformation."

The toolbox became my metaphor for growth, a way to understand how the small, consistent actions in our daily lives align with universal principles. Each tool I added wasn't random but purposeful, building on lessons learned and shaping my path forward. These tools helped me cultivate a sense of intention, guiding me toward a life of balance and alignment.

But the tools themselves didn't operate in isolation. They worked because they were rooted in a deeper understanding—one guided by the universal laws that govern all aspects of life.

These laws, though often invisible, influence our experiences, our energy, and even our outcomes. By aligning my actions with these principles, I found a sense of harmony and flow that made every step of the journey feel more intentional and impactful.

Through time and continued research sparked by curiosity, I began to uncover deeper truths about the world around me. At first, it was the small rituals—walking barefoot in the grass, making my bed each morning—that grounded me. But as I reflected on these practices, I found myself drawn to explore the forces that governed not just my actions, but the world itself.

This exploration led me to the work of Napoleon Hill, whose teachings became a cornerstone of my personal and professional growth. His set of books *The Law of Success in 16 Lessons* introduced me to principles that would shape my thinking for years to come. Hill's lessons on mindset, vision, and the power of thought taught me that success isn't a matter of luck, but a structured approach to life. His teachings made it clear that our thoughts shape our reality, and that alignment and intention are key to achieving our deepest desires.

Hill's work was like a gateway, leading me to other influential voices in the world of personal development. Bob Proctor, Earl Nightingale, and Abraham Hicks all built upon the foundation Hill had laid, each offering unique perspectives on the power of thought, vibration, and energy. They deepened my understanding of universal principles and provided tools that I could integrate into my life and my toolbox for transformation.

Hill's emphasis on alignment and intention naturally opened the door to the Universal Laws—laws that have always been present, shaping our experiences whether we're aware of them or not. These guiding forces influence not just our personal success but the very fabric of life itself. From the Law of

Attraction to the Law of Vibration, each law offers a unique perspective on how we interact with the world around us. These principles provided a framework for understanding how the universe operates and how we, as individuals, fit into this larger system.

What began as simple curiosity soon turned into a powerful framework for my own transformation. The more I aligned with these laws, the more my life began to flow with ease, purpose, and synchronicity. These laws weren't abstract ideas—they were practical tools that, when applied with intention, created real change in my life.

In this chapter, I'll introduce you to the 12 Universal Laws of Nature—the guiding principles that shape our existence and connect us to the world around us. These laws, like the tools in our toolbox, provide a framework for living in alignment with our highest selves. They are the unseen forces that, when understood and embraced, help us create a life of purpose, balance, and abundance.

As we explore each law, I'll share how they've influenced my journey and how you can incorporate them into your own life. Whether it's the Law of Vibration that reminds us everything is energy, or the Law of Correspondence that reflects our inner world in the external, these principles can guide you toward a more intentional and fulfilling life.

Through my experiences, I've learned that these laws are not static—they evolve with us. As we deepen our understanding of them, we continue to add new tools to our toolbox, discovering fresh ways to align with nature, nurture ourselves, and embrace the magic of transformation. Let's explore each of these Universal Laws and see how they can illuminate the path ahead.

1 The Law of Divine Oneness

At first, the idea that everything in the universe is connected felt too abstract for me. How could my small actions, my thoughts, or even my energy influence something so vast and intricate? But over time, as I began to reflect and dive deeper into this concept, it started to reveal itself in the simplest yet most profound ways.

I began to notice patterns. When I was in harmony—spending time in nature, practicing gratitude, or focusing on positivity— my relationships improved, and opportunities seemed to flow effortlessly. It felt as if the energy I was putting out into the world came back to me in unexpected and often beautiful ways. This realization taught me that I'm part of something much larger than myself, and that my actions, no matter how small, create ripples that extend far beyond my immediate awareness.

Understanding this law shifted how I approached every inter- action and decision. It wasn't just about me anymore—it was about the interconnections of everything. Each thought, word, or action held the potential to contribute to the greater whole, whether positively or negatively.

One of the ways I've embraced the Law of Divine Oneness is through giving. I've always believed in the profound impact of generosity, and as my financial situation improved, I was able to increase my contributions. While I aspire to one day be a great philanthropist, I've learned that even small acts of giving can create meaningful ripples. During times when money felt especially tight, I made it a point to give a little extra—not with the expectation of receiving in return, but to honor the flow of abundance.

For me, this practice wasn't about fixing my circumstances or seeking rewards; it was about reminding myself that scarcity is a mindset. Giving, even in small ways, felt like opening a door, allowing energy to flow freely rather than holding it back out of fear. Time and time again, I found that this act of generosity seemed to align me with abundance. Whether it was a raise, a bonus, or an unexpected financial opportunity, the flow would often return in ways I couldn't have predicted.

A good friend once shared a piece of wisdom with me that has stayed with me ever since: *Don't hold too tightly to money, because it restricts the flow in both directions.* Money, like energy, needs to circulate. When we hoard or cling to it out of fear, we create blockages that hinder both giving and receiving. But when we give freely, trusting that the universe will provide, we open ourselves to a cycle of abundance.

The Law of Divine Oneness has taught me that every act, no matter how small, carries significance. Whether it's a kind word, a thoughtful gesture, or a small donation, each action creates ripples that touch lives in ways we may never see. And the beauty of this law is that as we give, we also receive—not out of expectation, but as a natural result of aligning ourselves with the flow of the universe.

This understanding has been a cornerstone of my journey. It's a reminder that we're all connected, and that by nurturing this connection—through kindness, generosity, and mindfulness—we contribute to a world that's not just better for ourselves, but for everyone.

2 The Law of Vibration

The Law of Vibration became clear to me through practice and experimentation. I learned that everything—our thoughts, emotions, and actions—carries a frequency, a vibration that influences how we experience the world. As I began to observe how different activities or thoughts made me feel, it became evident that my vibration shaped the energy I attracted.

I noticed a significant shift when I started my day with positive rituals. Simple acts like making my bed or stepping outside for a moment of fresh air seemed to elevate my mood and set the tone for the rest of the day. These small, intentional actions lifted my vibration, and the day seemed to flow more smoothly. In contrast, when I let stress or negativity dominate my mornings, it felt like the world reflected that same energy back to me, creating obstacles and challenges.

As I explored this concept further, I became more intentional about raising my vibration. I discovered the power of sound and used YouTube videos specifically curated for their calming or uplifting effects. Whether it was nature sounds, affirmations, or motivational talks, these videos created an environment of positivity that influenced both me and my children. Starting the day with upbeat music became a cherished routine, one that still resonates with us. To this day, when any of us feels off balance, we often turn to music or sound as a way to shift our energy and perspective.

This practice reinforced what I'd come to understand about the Law of Vibration: the energy we cultivate within ourselves radiates outward, shaping our interactions and experiences. By consciously choosing thoughts, actions, and sounds that raise our frequency, we align ourselves with a higher vibration— one that attracts positivity, growth, and harmony. This simple yet powerful principle has become a cornerstone of my life, influencing not just how I begin my day, but how I navigate the world around me.

One of the most eye-opening ways the Law of Vibration reveals itself is through the reflection of your energy in those around you, especially your children. Children are like mirrors, sensitive to the moods, emotions, and vibrations we carry. I began to notice that when I was feeling down, stressed, or grouchy, my children's behavior would often shift to reflect that same energy. They would become irritable, clingy, or upset, almost as if they were absorbing what I was putting out.

Conversely, when I was intentional about maintaining a positive vibration—whether by starting the day with upbeat music, focusing on gratitude, or simply grounding myself—they responded in kind. Their laughter came more easily, their moods were brighter, and our interactions flowed with more harmony. It was a powerful reminder that our energy doesn't exist in a vacuum. It ripples out, affecting the people closest to us.

This realization became an important part of my daily practice. I understood that by consciously raising my own vibration, I wasn't just improving my own experience—I was creating a more positive environment for my children as well. It wasn't about being perfect or pretending to be happy when I wasn't, but about acknowledging my emotions and intentionally shifting my energy when I could. Sometimes, it meant taking a deep breath, going for a walk, or listening to calming music before engaging with them. Other times, it was as simple as sharing a laugh or a smile, knowing that those small moments had the power to change the energy in the room.

The beauty of this practice is that it's a two-way street. Just as my energy influences my children, their joy and positivity can also lift me up. The more aware I became of this dynamic, the more I realized the importance of cultivating a balanced and intentional vibration—not just for myself, but for the harmony of my family as a whole. It's a reminder that the energy we carry is not just ours; it's a gift we share with those around us.

3 The Law of Correspondence

"As above, so below; as within, so without."

The Law of Correspondence revealed itself to me in both subtle and striking ways. It taught me that the patterns I see in my life are often reflections of what's happening within me. Nature, my greatest teacher, illustrated this law beautifully: the way a still pond mirrors the sky, or how the seasons cycle in perfect rhythm. These patterns showed me that harmony within creates harmony without.

One of the most profound lessons in Correspondence came from observing my children. When I was feeling stressed or disconnected, their behavior would often mirror my energy—restless, irritable, or unsettled. On the other hand, when I was calm, grounded, and present, they reflected that back to me with laughter, cooperation, and joy. It was as though they held up a mirror to my internal state, teaching me to cultivate peace within to foster peace around me.

Similarly, I saw this mirrored in the workplace. As a manager, I observed how my mood could influence an entire team. If I showed up frustrated or disconnected, the group dynamic often became tense and unproductive. But when I entered the room grounded, optimistic, and focused, my energy elevated the team's morale and cohesiveness. It became clear that leadership wasn't just about words or actions—it was about *alignment*.

Over time, I also learned the importance of entering meetings or discussions with an open mind, especially when I felt uncertain or nervous about the outcome. When I walked into a situation already bracing for conflict or disappointment, it often seemed to materialize exactly that way. It was as though my expectations—born of fear or apprehension—subconsciously shaped my energy, my words, and even my body language, leading to the very result I hoped to avoid.

But when I intentionally shifted to an open and curious mindset, the dynamic would often change entirely. Instead of approaching the meeting with a rigid idea of how it might unfold, I focused on staying present, listening, and allowing the conversation to flow. By doing so, I found that I created space for solutions, collaboration, and even unexpected outcomes that were far better than I could have imagined.

This wasn't just about being optimistic; it was about letting go of the need to control every detail and trusting the process. The more open-minded and grounded I became, the more I noticed that others responded in kind. People felt heard, ideas flowed more freely, and tensions often dissipated before they even took hold.

One of the key lessons I took away from these experiences was that trying to predict or control an outcome can sometimes backfire. When we walk into a situation expecting conflict, we unconsciously set the stage for it. Our tone, posture, and even subtle cues reflect our inner state, and others pick up on that energy. But when we approach with openness, curiosity, and the intention to understand rather than to defend, we invite the possibility of connection and alignment.

This practice of openness didn't just help me navigate challenging conversations—it also became a cornerstone of my leadership philosophy. It taught me to trust both myself and the team, to release unnecessary fears, and to focus on creating an environment where collaboration could thrive.

The Law of Correspondence was at work here, too: as I adjusted my mindset and energy, I noticed those changes reflected in the room. Meetings that once felt tense or unproductive became opportunities for growth and understanding. And even when outcomes weren't exactly as I'd hoped, I found peace in knowing that I had approached the situation with integrity and intention.

Applying Correspondence Across Life

Recognizing the power of correspondence, I've adopted practices to align my internal world with the results I seek externally. For me, this means tuning into the message my mind and body are sending and adjusting accordingly:

- **Building Strength:** When I need to feel strong or face challenges, I prioritize strength training. Each repetition reminds me of my inner resilience and helps me carry that energy into my interactions.
- **Finding Flexibility:** When life feels rigid, or I sense a need to be more open, I turn to yoga. Stretching my body teaches me to stretch my mind, opening myself to new possibilities.
- **Restoring Calm:** When I feel scattered, meditation, a gentle walk in nature, or a long bath centers me. These moments of stillness ripple outward, helping me approach life's demands with clarity and balance.
- **Celebrating Energy:** On days I feel joy or excitement, I let it flow through movement—fast-paced walks, dancing, or celebrating the moment with a burst of energy. These

practices amplify the positivity I want to share with the world.

The Wisdom of Nature

Nature has always been my greatest teacher. The Law of Correspondence reveals itself in every corner of the natural world: the harmony of seasons, the balance between predators and prey, the way the roots of a tree mirror its branches above. This wisdom reminds me that everything is connected—what we nurture within, we nurture in the world around us.

By aligning my internal state with the outcomes I wish to see, I've discovered a sense of peace and flow that feels effortless. Life isn't always perfect, but the more I honor the Law of Correspondence, the more aligned my journey becomes.

Takeaways for the Reader

To align with the Law of Correspondence in your life:

1. **Notice Patterns:** Reflect on how your inner world influences your relationships, work, and daily experiences.
2. **Choose Practices Intentionally:** Align your actions with the energy you want to create—whether it's calm, strength, or joy.
3. **Embrace Nature as a Guide:** Look to nature for reminders of balance, harmony, and flow.

Life mirrors what we carry within. By nurturing our internal state, we create a ripple effect that transforms not just ourselves but the world around us.

4 The Law of Attraction

The Law of Attraction was one of the first universal laws I encountered, though I didn't fully understand its depth at the time. Early on, I thought it was simply about "thinking positively" and waiting for good things to happen. But as I explored it further, I came to realize that it wasn't just about thoughts. It was about aligning my feelings, beliefs, and actions with those thoughts to create the outcomes I desired.

One of the most profound lessons I learned about the Law of Attraction is that it's not just about wanting something; it's about becoming the kind of person who attracts it. It's about embodying the energy of what you want, even before it arrives. I've witnessed this law in action so many times in my life, from major milestones to the smallest synchronicities that left me in awe.

Manifestations in My Life

Looking back, I realize I've manifested so many incredible experiences, relationships, and opportunities—both consciously and unconsciously. One of my favorite examples is the job I manifested that I could walk to. I had always dreamed of being able to walk to work, but for a long time, it seemed like a far-off fantasy. Then, just as I began to feel stale and disconnected in my current role, the perfect opportunity appeared. It wasn't just coincidence—it was a result of my long-held desire aligning with my energy at that moment.

I also manifested my family life. My children, my husband, and the beautiful relationships we've built didn't come by accident. I believe the love and intention I put into the universe came back to me in the form of the family I had always dreamed of. Similarly, I manifested the property with the pond—a place that feels like a reflection of my inner peace and connection with nature. It's a space I didn't just stumble upon; it's a vision I held in my heart long before it became a reality.

Even when my focus wasn't entirely clear, the Law of Attraction still worked. For instance, I wasn't particularly happy in the job I was promoted into. While it brought the financial increase I was focused on, it also created conflict with my deeper desire to spend more time with my children and take care of my home. It felt misaligned with what I truly valued, but at the time, I was singularly focused on money—and the universe delivered exactly what I was asking for.

While the job wasn't the perfect long-term fit, it served as a stepping stone. It taught me a valuable lesson about being specific and intentional with what I want—not just in terms of material gains, but also how I want to feel and grow along the way. That experience reminded me that clarity is essential when working with the Law of Attraction. It's not just about asking for something tangible; it's about aligning with the bigger picture of how I want my life to look and feel.

When the timing was just right, I was let go of that job. At first, it felt unexpected and unsettling, but with time, I came to see it as a gift. The space it created in my life opened the door to something far greater. Eventually, again when the timing was just right, I found a position that offered all the flexibility I craved—a role that aligns beautifully with both my personal and professional values. This shift wasn't just a coincidence; it was the universe working in harmony with the intentions I had set, even if I hadn't realized it at the time.

This experience solidified my belief in the power of the Law of Attraction. It reminded me to trust the process and to release attachment to the "how." Sometimes, what feels like a setback is actually the universe paving the way for something better. By aligning my thoughts, feelings, and actions with my true desires, I've learned that life unfolds in ways that not only fulfill our immediate needs but also bring us closer to our most authentic selves.

And then there are the countless smaller manifestations I've lost track of—unexpected gifts, opportunities, or even the perfect timing of a phone call or message. These moments remind me that the Law of Attraction isn't just about the "big" things. It's a constant flow of energy, always responding to what we put out into the world.

How the Law Works in My Life

The more I worked with the Law of Attraction, the clearer it became: it's not just about thinking positively; it's about feeling aligned with the outcome. Gratitude has been one of the most powerful tools for me. When I focused on what I was already grateful for, more things to be grateful for seemed to appear. It was as if the universe matched my vibration, sending more experiences that aligned with the energy of gratitude and abundance.

Action is another key piece of this law. It's not enough to just think about what you want; you have to take inspired steps toward it. Whether it's reaching out to someone, taking a class, or simply saying "yes" to an opportunity that feels right, action creates momentum. It signals to the universe that you're serious about your intentions and ready to receive.

Lessons From Manifesting

What I've learned from working with the Law of Attraction is that we are always manifesting—whether we realize it or not. Our thoughts, emotions, and actions are constantly creating our reality. When we focus on scarcity or fear, we attract more of the same. But when we focus on abundance, joy, and possibility, the universe reflects that back to us in ways we often can't predict.

This law has taught me to be intentional with my energy, to trust the timing of my desires, and to let go of the "how." Some of the best manifestations in my life came in ways I never could have planned. It's a reminder that the universe has a far greater perspective than I do, and when I align my energy with my intentions, I can trust that things will unfold perfectly—even if they don't look exactly the way I imagined.

The Power of the Law of Attraction: Fueling Success for All

One of the most profound truths I've come to embrace is the power of the Law of Attraction. It's a reminder that our thoughts, intentions, and beliefs shape the reality around us. When we focus on abundance, positivity, and success, we naturally attract more of it into our lives. But this isn't just a solo journey—each person's individual success adds fuel to the success of others.

Imagine a world where we are all cheerleaders for each other, celebrating every small win and every major breakthrough. When we support and lift each other up, we create a ripple effect that magnifies success on a much larger scale. There is no limit to the abundance the universe has to offer. There are infinite resources—enough for everyone to thrive.

The more we align ourselves with this mindset, the more we become magnets for success, joy, and prosperity. And when one of us succeeds, we all do. Together, we create a network of energy that flows with the power of positivity, uplifting not just ourselves, but everyone we come into contact with.

Final Reflection

The Law of Attraction is real. It's a constant force that shapes our lives, whether we're aware of it or not. By aligning our thoughts, feelings, and actions with our desires, we have the power to co-create a reality that reflects our highest intentions. My journey with this law has been nothing short of magical, and it continues to remind me that we are always creating—moment by moment, thought by thought.

5 The Law of Inspired Action

While the Law of Attraction emphasizes focusing on what we want, the Law of Inspired Action reminds us that we must take meaningful steps toward those desires. Without action, intentions remain just that—intentions.

Inspired action isn't about simply "doing for the sake of doing." It's about aligning with your intuition and moving forward when the timing feels right. For me, this became clear during moments of reflection. When I listened to that inner voice—whether it nudged me to start a new project, step back and rest, or shift my focus entirely—the universe responded in powerful ways. It was the small, inspired steps that often led to the most profound opportunities and transformations.

But what about those times when the path forward feels unclear, or the energy to take action seems to be missing? That's when I lean into my wellness rituals. For me, wellness has always been a placeholder for inspired action, a way to keep energy flowing when life feels stagnant or directionless. These rituals help me re-calibrate, and often, they lead to clarity and momentum in surprising ways.

- **Deep Breathing**: When my mind feels cluttered or over-whelmed, a few minutes of intentional, deep breathing can shift my energy completely. Each inhale feels like a reset button, and each exhale releases tension, opening up space for new thoughts and ideas to flow.
- **Stretching**: Sometimes, simply stretching my body is enough to wake up my spirit. The gentle movement not only eases physical tightness but also reminds me of the importance of flexibility—in both body and mind.
- **Change of Scenery**: When inspiration feels far away, step-ping outside or moving to a new environment can work wonders. Whether it's a walk through nature, sitting by the water, or even just changing rooms, the shift often sparks fresh perspectives and ideas.
- **Walking**: There's something magical about the rhythm of walking. It's like the movement creates a natural flow of energy and thought. Some of my clearest moments of inspiration have come while taking a walk, letting my mind wander in sync with my steps.
- **Napping**: Rest is often undervalued, but it's a key part of renewal for me. A short nap can be a bridge between stuck energy and inspired energy. I often wake up with a clearer mind and a renewed sense of purpose.

Each of these practices is simple but powerful. They help me reconnect with myself, tune into my intuition, and prepare for the inspired action that's just around the corner. Wellness rituals don't just fill the gap between moments of clarity and action—they create the conditions for clarity and action to emerge.

When I feel lost or unsure of the next step, I know I can always return to these rituals. They ground me, energize me, and remind me that action—when aligned with intuition—is the key to creating meaningful change. Wellness becomes the bridge between intention and action, holding space until the next inspired step appears.

6 The Law of Perpetual Transmutation of Energy

This law taught me a powerful truth: energy is always in motion, and we have the ability to transform it. It reminded me that no matter how heavy or stagnant a situation may feel, I don't have to stay in that state. With small, intentional actions, I can shift the energy around me and create something new—something lighter, more positive, and more aligned with how I want to feel.

One of the most profound ways I've embraced this law is through my bath rituals. Stepping into the warm water feels like stepping into a sanctuary. As I soak, I visualize the day's stress dissolving, allowing the water to carry it away. Each ingredient I add—Epsom salt for grounding, cinnamon for warmth and comfort, coconut oil for nourishment—has its own purpose, creating an experience of release and renewal. These moments of intentional care remind me that I always have the power to shift my energy and transform my experience.

But what I've come to realize is that this law works just as powerfully in the smallest, simplest acts of everyday life. When life feels overwhelming or energy feels stuck, I've learned to lean into tiny, meaningful actions to start the process of change.

- **A Shared Smile or Laughter**: Sometimes, all it takes is a genuine smile or a laugh to begin shifting the energy. Sharing a lighthearted moment with someone—even a stranger—has a way of breaking through the tension and creating warmth.
- **Cleaning and Decluttering**: Physical spaces carry energy too, and cleaning or decluttering a room can feel like a reset button for my mind. Reorganizing a drawer or clearing a surface not only creates order but also opens space for fresh energy to flow.
- **Essential Oils and Aromatherapy**: Scents have a profound ability to influence mood. A few drops of lavender can bring calm, while citrus oils uplift and energize. Lighting a candle or diffusing a favorite oil can create an immediate shift in the atmosphere.
- **Baking or Cooking**: There's something magical about creating something with your hands. Baking a batch of cookies or preparing a nourishing meal feels grounding and joyful, and the act itself becomes a form of care—for myself and for others.
- **Reading or Writing**: Escaping into a good book or jotting down thoughts in a journal has a way of calming my mind and sparking new ideas. Both are simple yet powerful ways to change the energy in my day.
- **Reaching Out to a Friend**: Sometimes, the quickest way to transform energy is through connection. A heartfelt conversation, even just a quick text to check in with someone I care about, reminds me of the support and love that

surrounds me.

· **Acts of Kindness**: Doing something kind for someone else—a small good deed or a thoughtful gesture—shifts the focus away from my own stress and creates a ripple of positivity.

What I've come to love about this law is how accessible it is. While larger rituals like my bath practice are deeply trans-formative, the small, everyday actions are just as powerful. Each tiny shift builds on the one before, creating momentum that changes not only my energy but the energy of those around me.

This law is a beautiful reminder that even when life feels out of control, I always have the ability to start where I am, with what I have, and create a shift. Energy is constantly moving, and with a little intention, I can guide it in a direction that brings peace, joy, and inspiration.

7 The Law of Cause and Effect

Over time, I began to witness how the Law of Cause and Effect wove through my life. Often summed up as "what you sow, you reap," this law illuminated a profound truth: every action, no matter how small, has a consequence. Sometimes those effects were immediate, like a warm smile in response to a kind word. Other times, the results unfolded slowly, like seeds planted in a garden that would eventually bloom.

This awareness transformed the way I approached my choices. It taught me to be mindful of the energy I carried and the intentions behind my actions, knowing that what I sent out into the world would, in time, find its way back to me. Positivity is contagious—but so is negativity. I came to see that my thoughts, words, and actions didn't just shape my day; they rippled outward, affecting others and creating the conditions for future experiences.

Mindfulness became my guide. When I approached the world with kindness, patience, and a dedication to my well-being, I noticed how these values began to shape my reality. My relationships deepened, opportunities flowed more freely, and challenges felt easier to navigate. These ripples of positive energy were a direct reflection of the intentions I set and the actions I took.

But this law is not about perfection—it's about awareness. Like all of the universal laws, it requires patience and practice. It's easy to fall into self-criticism when things don't go as planned or when we catch ourselves acting out of alignment. The key is to be kind to yourself in those moments. Growth is not linear, and transformation is a journey, not a destination.

I learned to hold myself accountable without being unduly harsh. Mistakes became opportunities to reflect, adjust, and grow. With time, I began to see how mindfulness and awareness brought clarity to my actions and their effects. I became more attuned to how I influenced my circumstances, both positively and negatively, and this awareness empowered me to make intentional choices that aligned with my values.

The beauty of the Law of Cause and Effect lies in its simplicity: what you give, you get. But it's also a powerful reminder that we are all co-creators of our reality. Each choice we make, each energy we carry, sets a ripple in motion. And with patience, practice, and compassion for ourselves, we can guide those ripples to create a life that reflects the very best of who we are.

8 The Law of Compensation

As I embraced the Law of Compensation, I came to understand that the universe is constantly working to balance the scales. This law reassured me that the energy and effort we put into the world always return to us, though often in ways we might not anticipate. It taught me that everything has a rhythm, a natural balance that ensures what we give is matched by what we receive.

I began noticing the law in subtle but meaningful ways—a kind gesture repaid with unexpected opportunities, moments of generosity leading to deeper connections, or even the quiet fulfillment that comes from knowing I'm living in alignment with my values. These weren't always direct exchanges, but they always felt like reminders that the universe sees and rewards our intentions, even when it feels like no one else does.

The imagery of a scale helped me visualize this law in action. Each choice we make and each action we take adds weight to one side of the scale. It's easy to let negativity, frustration, or doubt tip the balance in ways we don't want, but the beauty of the Law of Compensation is that we always have the ability to realign. By tipping the scales toward positivity—through kindness, gratitude, and trust—we invite the universe to respond in kind.

This law also taught me that compensation isn't just about what we offer to others—it's also about how we treat ourselves. Compassion and kindness toward ourselves can create a shift that promotes positivity from within, radiating outward to touch every aspect of our lives. When I forgive myself for mistakes, acknowledge my efforts, and allow myself moments of rest and reflection, I find that my energy naturally realigns. This self-compassion becomes its own reward, creating a ripple effect of peace and confidence that extends to those around me.

The Law of Compensation encourages us to trust that what we

put into the world and into ourselves will come back to us. It's not about perfection or grand gestures but about sincerity and consistency. Even the smallest acts—whether offering a smile to a stranger or taking a quiet moment to appreciate our own journey—can tip the scales toward balance and abundance.

When I feel like the scales aren't balancing, I reflect on where I might need to shift my energy. Am I holding onto negativity? Am I giving without boundaries, or am I not giving enough? Am I neglecting to show myself the same compassion I extend to others? By paying attention to these questions, I can make small but intentional adjustments to keep the balance tipping toward the positive.

Ultimately, this law has taught me to trust the flow of energy and effort in my life. It has shown me that everything—every action, every thought, every choice—creates ripples that eventually return to me. By focusing on the good I can contribute both outwardly and inwardly, I know the scales will always tip in favor of fulfillment, abundance, and joy.

9 The Law of Relativity

The Law of Relativity taught me that everything is relative to our perspective. What may seem like a challenge to one person could be an opportunity for growth to another. Through my own experiences, I began to see that shifting my perspective could completely change how I viewed obstacles.

One of the most powerful ways I embraced this law was by adopting the simple mindset of "I get to." Instead of feeling burdened by daily responsibilities, I began to see them as privileges.

- *I get to go to work*—an opportunity to contribute and grow.
- *I get to do the laundry*—a chance to care for my family and enjoy the comforts of a home.
- *I get to do the grocery shopping*—a way to care for my family and nourish those I love.
- *I get to take the car for an oil change*—a reminder that I have a car to take care of and the means to keep it running smoothly.
- *I get to drive the kids to their activities*—a chance to share hidden moments of connection, free of distractions and pressure. This became one of my favorites, as those moments were fleeting and I was fully aware of that.

This subtle shift re-frames even the most mundane tasks into gifts. It allows us to recognize the opportunities hidden within what we might otherwise overlook. What once felt like an obligation began to feel like a privilege.

When faced with difficult situations, I started asking myself: *What can I learn from this? What is this teaching me?* This curiosity opened the door to gratitude, even during tough times. Every experience became a stepping stone, building resilience and shaping my perspective.

By practicing the "I get to" mindset, I realized that opportunities for growth, connection, and gratitude are everywhere. The Law of Relativity became a reminder to embrace life's contrasts, seeing each moment for what it is: a chance to grow, learn, and thrive.

It's not about erasing the challenges but shifting the lens through which we see them. Every "I get to" moment holds the potential for a profound transformation.

10 The Law of Polarity

The Law of Polarity reminded me that everything in life has its opposite—joy and sorrow, light and dark, abundance and lack. By embracing the full spectrum of emotions and experiences, I discovered a deeper sense of balance and understanding.

Instead of resisting life's lows, I began to see them as essential parts of the natural cycle. This shift in perspective allowed me to move through difficult times with greater grace and peace. The more I embraced the contrasts, the more I recognized the lessons they carried.

Rejection, for instance, often opened new doors I hadn't noticed before. What seemed like a setback at first became an opportunity for growth, redirection, and clarity. Losing a loved one brought immense grief, but it also deepened my gratitude for the time we shared together and the memories we created. I learned that even loss carries a kind of bittersweet beauty, reminding me to cherish every moment.

One of the most profound lessons came when I lost my long-standing job. Initially, the change felt overwhelming and uncertain, but it created space for something much greater—time with my family when it was most needed. It became a season of focus, healing, and connection, one that I never would have fully embraced without the shift that loss created.

Watching my children grow has been another poignant reminder of polarity. Each stage of their development feels like a constant goodbye to yesterday, as they step into who they are becoming. While there's a wistful longing for the past, there's also immense joy and pride in witnessing their growth and evolution.

The Law of Polarity taught me to look for the lessons hidden within life's contrasts. It encouraged me to hold space for both the joy and the sorrow, the gain and the loss. By accepting and even embracing both sides of life, I found a deeper fulfillment and understanding.

This law reminded me that life isn't about avoiding challenges or clinging to one side of the spectrum—it's about appreciating the full tapestry. Each thread, whether dark or light, contributes to the richness of the journey. When we honor the lessons of polarity, we move closer to balance, resilience, and a profound sense of gratitude for the beauty of it all.

11 The Law of Rhythm

The Law of Rhythm taught me to embrace the natural cycles of life. Just as the seasons change, so do the phases of our lives. I learned to honor these rhythms, allowing myself to rest when needed and to take action when the time felt right.

This law became a profound teacher of patience and trust. In slower phases, when progress felt stagnant or uncertain, I reminded myself that everything would shift in time. By aligning with life's natural rhythms, I began to flow with ease, recognizing that each phase had its own unique purpose—even if its purpose wasn't clear in the moment.

This past year has been a particularly powerful example of this law in action. Losing my long-standing job was a shock. It was a cornerstone for my family, providing stability and predictability, and not something I would have chosen to give up on my own. However, when the decision was made for me, I leaned into the change rather than resisting it.

What I didn't know at the time was how perfectly this shift in rhythm would align with life's greater plan. That unexpected loss of work gave me the time, energy, and focus I needed to be fully present for my family during one of the most challenging periods we've faced. A family health crisis emerged shortly after, and I was able to step into the role of caregiver without the added strain of balancing a demanding job.

Looking back, it's clear to me now how beautifully the rhythm of life unfolded. The slower season of letting go of my career transitioned into an active season of care, growth, and connection with my loved ones. Had I clung to resistance or fear, I might have missed the blessings hidden within this challenging time.

The Law of Rhythm reminds us that every phase—whether restful or active, challenging or abundant—serves a purpose in the larger flow of our lives. When we learn to trust the rhythm, to embrace the shifts and cycles, we open ourselves to unexpected blessings and find peace in knowing that life always moves forward.

12 The Law of Gender

The final law, the Law of Gender, taught me the importance of balancing masculine and feminine energies within myself. These energies are not about gender identity but about the qualities they represent: the masculine embodies strength, action, and logic, while the feminine encompasses creativity, intuition, and stillness. I began to see how both were necessary for growth, fulfillment, and alignment.

This law helped me realize that life is not about constantly pushing forward or endlessly resting—true harmony comes from knowing when to act with purpose and when to pause and reflect. By nurturing both sides—taking action when needed and embracing rest when called for—I discovered a rhythm that felt more aligned with who I am.

I learned that strength and resilience are invaluable when challenges arise, but so is the quiet power of reflection. For example, there were times when forging ahead with determination was the only way to overcome obstacles. But there were also moments when stepping back, allowing creativity to flow, or simply resting, provided the clarity I needed to move forward with greater purpose.

This balance became a guiding force in my life. When I felt the urge to create, I gave myself permission to let ideas take shape naturally, whether through writing, problem-solving, or simply daydreaming. When I felt the pull to rest, I trusted that rest was not a sign of weakness but an essential part of the process—a time to renew, recharge, and prepare for the next phase of action.

Awareness became key. The more I tuned into what I truly needed in any given moment, the more purposeful my actions became. Instead of acting out of habit or pressure, I began moving with intention, trusting my intuition to guide me toward the next step.

The Law of Gender reminds us that life is a dance between action and reflection, strength and stillness, logic and intuition. By honoring both masculine and feminine energies within ourselves, we create a sense of wholeness—a life that feels complete, balanced, and deeply fulfilling.

True power lies in embracing both sides. Take inspired action when the time is right, rest when your body and mind need it, and allow creativity to flow when inspiration strikes. This balance doesn't just bring harmony; it brings alignment with your truest self, creating a life of purpose, growth, and beauty.

Conclusion: Curiosity and Alignment

As I continued to explore these laws through both research and experience, I realized that living in alignment with the universe is not a destination but a journey—one sparked by curiosity and guided by intentional practice. What began as small, personal rituals of self-care grew into a deeper understanding of how the world works at a fundamental level. The Universal Laws, once abstract concepts, became the invisible forces that shaped my life, transforming not just my mindset, but my reality.

The beauty of this journey is that it isn't about perfection or mastering all of the laws at once. It's about remaining open, curious, and willing to explore how these principles show up in our everyday lives. Each day presents new opportunities to apply these laws—to witness their effects in small moments, to learn from them, and to adjust our approach accordingly. There is no rush; the universe is patient, allowing us to learn and grow at our own pace.

Curiosity was my compass throughout this process, leading me from one discovery to the next. It invited me to question old beliefs, to dig deeper into my experiences, and to embrace the unknown with a sense of wonder. This curiosity opened the door to a greater understanding of how the Universal Laws were already at work in my life, even before I knew them by name.

I began to see that aligning with these laws wasn't about controlling outcomes but about co-creating with the universe. It was about trusting the flow, knowing that when I acted with intention and faith, the universe would meet me halfway. It was about releasing the need for instant results and instead embracing the process—allowing each law to guide me through both the highs and lows of life with grace.

As I integrated these laws into my daily life, I found that challenges became less daunting, and opportunities began to present themselves in unexpected ways. By aligning with the Law of Rhythm, I learned to trust the natural ebb and flow of life. Through the Law of Polarity, I found balance in embracing both joy and sorrow. With the Law of Compensation, I came to understand that every effort, every moment of growth, is always rewarded—even if the reward comes in a form I didn't expect.

Ultimately, this journey is about deepening our relationship with ourselves and the world around us. It's about recognizing that we are part of something much larger, and that by aligning with these universal truths, we can live a life of greater purpose, peace, and abundance. The 12 Universal Laws offer us a framework—not just for personal transformation, but for living in harmony with the energies that shape our reality.

This chapter of my life is still unfolding, and I remain committed to the path of curiosity and alignment. Each day brings new lessons, new challenges, and new opportunities to align more deeply with these laws. And as I continue to walk this path, I know that the universe will continue to guide me, offering wisdom and support at every turn.

For those reading this, my hope is that you too will embrace this journey with curiosity. Let these laws serve as a compass for your own growth, and trust that as you align with them, the universe will respond in ways that are both magical and transformative. The path ahead is not always clear, but with each step you take in alignment with these laws, you move closer to the life you are meant to live.

3

Chapter 3

The Power of Influence and Meditation

It was through Napoleon Hill's work that I first discovered Bob Proctor. His videos on YouTube opened the door to a deeper understanding of Hill's teachings. But what stood out most was Proctor's emphasis on meditation, something I had read about countless times before but never fully embraced. Despite the wealth of advice encouraging me to meditate, it wasn't until I watched Bob Proctor that I felt truly compelled to start the practice.

Proctor made it feel accessible, like something I was capable of incorporating into my daily life. His calm and deliberate way of explaining the power of the mind through meditation resonated with me in a way that no other source had. It wasn't about forcing myself into quiet, but about aligning with the natural rhythm of my thoughts and energy. That shift in perspective made all the difference.

I often let my mind wander during meditation, and that's perfectly okay. Meditation is something I wholeheartedly recommend, although I admit I don't fully understand its power. What I do know is that it is powerful.

When you sit and practice, the goal isn't to force your mind into silence—it's to let yourself be. If thoughts keep coming, let them. Acknowledge them, and then let them go. Don't judge yourself for how long your mind stays busy or how often your thoughts drift. Just gently move on. Sit for as long as you can, and keep trying.

The true essence of meditation, I've found, is self-compassion. It's about giving yourself permission to not get it "right" every time. The idea is to feel good—if it starts to feel forceful or uncomfortable, that's okay too. Just try again another time.

Meditation isn't about perfection. It's about showing up, practicing, and learning to allow what is.

As I continued to meditate, I was introduced to Abraham Hicks' teachings, which further deepened my practice. Hicks' focus on vibrational alignment and the power of deliberate thought became essential to my daily routine. Together, Proctor and Hicks helped me create a meditation practice that wasn't just about stillness, but about actively shaping my reality through focus and intention.

This combination of influence turned meditation into something far more powerful than I could have imagined. It became a way to connect with myself, tune into my desires, and manifest my goals with clarity. It's a practice I return to again and again, knowing that it has the ability to transform not just my mind, but my life.

The Magic of Alignment

There have been moments in my life when things I'd been hoping for began to appear, almost as if by magic. Often, these blessings arrived in ways I hadn't anticipated, so I didn't recognize them immediately. One of the most magical parts of the vortex is that it holds not only the desires I consciously ask for but also the ones I may not even realize I need. Once, while working on manifesting greater abundance, I focused intently on a specific financial goal. I took action, maintained alignment as best I could, and soon, opportunities began to unfold. But what truly surprised me were the unexpected paths— opportunities I hadn't thought to ask for. A new connection, a beautiful experience shared with family, a stroke of good luck. Each one arrived with perfect timing, as if orchestrated to add richness to my life in ways I hadn't considered.

This is the magic of alignment. The vortex doesn't just hold what I think I want—it holds what's best for me, even when I may not yet know to ask for it.

The Vortex: Holding the Dreams We've Yet to Realize

I see the Vortex as a sacred space, a place where all my dreams and desires reside, waiting for me to align with them. In this place, every wish, every goal I've ever had is already fulfilled— existing in perfect harmony, ready to flow into my life when I'm vibrationally aligned. The Vortex is more than a concept; it's a dynamic container of possibility, holding not just the things I've consciously asked for, but also the dreams I haven't fully realized yet.

In Abraham Hicks' teachings, the Vortex is often described as a state of vibrational alignment, where everything you desire already exists. For me, this has been a place of reassurance and excitement. The more I step into alignment, the more I feel those desires begin to manifest in unexpected and beautiful ways. It's not about forcing or chasing; it's about allowing. The Vortex is always there, holding all that I hope for, even when I can't see it clearly.

This connection to the Vortex makes the journey feel magical. It's a reminder that life unfolds in its own perfect timing, and everything I desire is not only possible but is waiting for me.

Personal Wellness Toolbox

In the journey toward well-being, there are times when we feel out of alignment—disconnected from the flow, from our center, or from the sense of ease that Abraham Hicks describes as "the vortex." These are the moments when we need a toolbox: a collection of simple yet powerful practices to bring us back into alignment. Each tool in this toolbox supports physical, mental, and emotional health, offering ways to reconnect, recharge, and return to that place of balance and inner harmony. Whether you turn to one practice or several, these tools are here to help you realign and rediscover the calm and clarity that are always within reach.

Deep Breathing

A few deep breaths can calm the nervous system and bring peace. Slowly inhale through the nose and exhale through the mouth, letting each breath ground you. At times, I've found YouTube videos helpful for guiding and keeping me on track. An added bonus—you've just completed a quick meditation!

Yoga

Yoga combines movement and mindfulness, helping you build strength, flexibility, and inner calm. Remember, no special mat is needed—just find a quiet space. Even a few simple poses can help you feel centered and renewed.

Going for a Walk

A short walk outside is wonderful, but even moving around indoors can lift your mood. A few simple squats can get the blood flowing and help reset both body and mind.

Light Stretches

Stretching can ease muscle tension and bring relaxation. The best part? Stretches can be done anywhere—at the office, on the couch, or even in your car. They're perfect for a quick reset.

Heavy Lifting

Lifting weights or doing body weight exercises like squats not only builds physical strength but can also be empowering. It's especially helpful when feeling weak or needing to work out extra energy. Strong body, strong mind.

Napping

Sometimes, you just don't have the energy for anything else. A short nap can restore focus and lift your mood. Adding pleasant background noise can make it easier to drift off and make the experience even more restful.

Talking with a Friend

Connection provides comfort and perspective. Sometimes, even a big smile shared with a stranger can work wonders. Reach out to someone you trust or bring a little positivity to a new interaction.

Baths

A warm bath relaxes muscles, promotes calm, and soothes the senses. Be creative with your time—baths don't have to be lengthy, though that can be an extra indulgence!

Music

Music can lift the spirit or help release tension. I recommend keeping playlists and switching things up depending on the moment. Music that fits your mood can make a world of difference.

Jokes & Funny Videos

Laughter is powerful, reducing stress and brightening your day. And don't be afraid to laugh out loud, especially if you're alone—it's a great way to feel uplifted instantly.

Good Memories

Reflecting on happy memories can shift your perspective to a more positive outlook. Look at old photos, revisit cherished moments, and allow yourself to relive those feelings of joy and gratitude.

These are the tools I've gathered along my journey—practices that ground, uplift, and help me realign. My toolbox continues to grow, shaped by new experiences, insights, and the changing seasons of life. Each tool has become a touchstone, a reminder of my commitment to well-being and resilience.

I encourage you to explore, experiment, and build a toolbox that fits you. What works best may shift depending on the moment or chapter of life, and that's the beauty of it. Find what resonates, let it evolve, and embrace the small rituals that bring you balance and joy. Your toolbox is uniquely yours, filled with whatever you need to support, nurture, and inspire yourself.

4

Chapter 4

The Vortex – A Space for Dreams and Alignment

The concept of the vortex first came to me through the teachings of Abraham Hicks. She introduced me to the idea that there's a space—a vortex—where all of my desires exist, waiting for me to align with them so they can manifest into my physical reality. Over time, my understanding of the vortex has evolved, and I've come to see it as a space where not only my intentional dreams reside, but also the ones I may not even be fully aware of. The vortex holds everything—my hopes, my desires, and even the things I haven't consciously asked for.

But just like Abraham Hicks teaches, the vortex responds to the energy we bring to it. That's why I've learned to be mindful of my thoughts and intentions. If I allow worry or negative thinking to dominate, it's as if I'm unintentionally pushing my dreams further away. The more I focus on what I don't want, the more I fuel the likelihood of those things coming into my reality. This is why staying in alignment, or finding ways to get back into alignment quickly, is so important.

The Power of Thought and Intention

One of the most pivotal moments in my journey was when I came across a video that completely shifted my perspective on worry. The video reminded me that worry, though it has its place, can also be a dangerous emotion. If you sit in it for too long, it becomes a form of resistance that pulls you out of alignment with your vortex.

This realization was both empowering and trans-formative. I understood that while worry can serve as a prompt to take action or make plans, I had to be careful not to dwell in that space. The key, I learned, is to acknowledge the worry, make a plan—no matter how small—and shift my energy as quickly as possible. By taking action, I can stop feeding the negative energy and begin moving forward in a positive direction.

Worry Has Its Place—But Don't Stay There

Worry is a natural part of life, and it's there to alert us when something needs our attention. However, I've learned that lingering in that space for too long hinders progress. When I catch myself worrying, I immediately try to take an action that will make me feel better—even if it's something simple. Anything that brings relief can work. Sometimes, it's as basic as doing the dishes to feel accomplished, taking a walk, or even eating a piece of chocolate, get your "toolbox". The key is that whatever you do, it has to genuinely make you feel better.

Taking action helps shift the energy, which in turn helps realign me with the vortex. With practice, I've found that small, meaningful actions help me regain that sense of flow.

Positive Forward Movement—The Key to Staying in Alignment

The quicker I can take action, the quicker I can realign with the vortex. I've found that when I shift my focus from fear to positive, forward movement, everything feels lighter. It's as though I'm signaling to the universe, "I'm ready for things to work out," and that's when the magic happens. I become a magnet for solutions, opportunities, and the fulfillment of my dreams.

This doesn't mean I expect perfection from myself. We all have moments when worry or fear gets the best of us. What matters is recognizing those moments and then making a conscious choice to move forward. The key is in the small steps that shift your focus, bringing you closer to alignment each time.

We Are Not Perfect—But We Can Keep Moving Forward

Perfection isn't the goal. Part of this journey is learning to show myself grace. When I slip into worry or doubt, I know it's a temporary state, not a reflection of my overall progress. The important thing is that I recognize when I'm out of alignment and take the steps to shift my energy.

Self-compassion is a crucial part of this. I've learned that falling out of alignment isn't a failure—it's an opportunity to grow stronger in my ability to realign. Each time I catch myself and shift, I'm reinforcing my ability to return to the vortex more easily in the future.

Manifesting Dreams from the Vortex into Physical Reality

When I'm aligned, I've seen amazing things happen. Dreams and desires that have been waiting in the vortex begin to show up in my life, often in ways that feel magical. Sometimes, they are things I've actively worked toward, but other times, they are beautiful surprises—dreams I didn't even realize I had.

This is the magic of the vortex: it holds everything I've ever wanted, even those desires that have formed quietly and subconsciously. When I'm aligned, the vortex reveals them to me in the perfect timing.

Trust the Process and Yourself

The most important lesson I've learned is to trust—trust in the process of alignment, trust in the timing of the universe, and trust in myself. I know that I won't always stay perfectly aligned, but I have the tools to come back to center. The beauty is in knowing that with every small shift, every mindful action, I'm moving closer to the vortex, where everything I desire is waiting for me.

5

Chapter 5

Turning Negativity into Positive Energy

Life will inevitably present us with challenges and negativity, whether they stem from external situations or our own internal thoughts. While we can't control everything that happens around us, we can always control how we respond. This is one of the most trans-formative lessons I've learned, and it's one I continue to practice daily. The power lies in choosing not to stay in negativity but to consciously shift the energy toward something positive.

Embracing Change as a Gift

One of the most profound ways I experienced this transfor-mation was during a time of unexpected loss. When I lost my long-standing job, it felt as if the ground beneath me had shifted. This position had provided stability and predictability for my family, and its sudden absence could have easily left me in a state of fear and worry. But instead of staying in that space, I made a conscious decision to embrace the time I'd been given.

Even before I understood the full significance of this newfound time, I treated it as a gift. I used the quiet days to focus on wellness, reconnect with myself, and prepare for whatever might come next. What I couldn't have known then was that life was aligning me for something far more important. Shortly after, my son faced a major health crisis that required our full attention. Without the demands of a job pulling me in different directions, I was able to be fully present for him—physically, emotionally, and mentally—during every hospital visit, every decision, and every moment of hope and uncertainty.

Even before we knew what the outcome would be, I cherished the time we spent together. In a "normal" life, we both would have been consumed by work and daily demands, leaving little room for these quiet, meaningful connections. But during this period, I found immense gratitude for the time we had, even amid the challenges. It was a powerful reminder that even in life's hardest moments, there is beauty to be found.

When his recovery began, the nature of our time together shifted. The quiet worry that had lingered was replaced with celebration and joy. Watching him heal and thrive was a gift I didn't take for granted, and I relished every moment of it. I truly believe that focusing on positivity—even in uncertainty—helped create an environment where hope and resilience could thrive.

The Power of Perspective

This experience taught me that in every situation, we have a choice. While we may not be able to change our circumstances, we can always change how we respond. By looking for the positive, even in the smallest ways, we can shift the energy around us. That shift doesn't just impact our own mindset—it ripples outward, affecting the people we love and the outcomes we create.

Negativity can feel overwhelming, but it's rarely as permanent as it seems in the moment. The key is to focus on what's within our control. When negativity begins to creep in, I turn to the tools that have become part of my daily life. These aren't elaborate practices—they're small, accessible actions that help create meaningful shifts.

Tools for Transforming Energy

1. **Deep Breathing**: A few intentional breaths can calm the mind and body. With each inhale, I invite peace, and with each exhale, I release tension.
2. **Yoga or Stretching**: Moving through tension physically helps release it emotionally. Yoga connects me with my body and restores balance.
3. **A Walk in Nature**: Stepping outside clears my head and reconnects me with the grounding energy of the earth.
4. **Reaching Out to a Friend**: Talking with someone who understands can lighten the load and provide new perspectives.
5. **Journaling or Reflecting**: Writing down my thoughts allows me to process emotions and often leads to unexpected insights.
6. **Acts of Kindness**: Doing something kind for someone else shifts my focus outward and reminds me of the positive impact I can have.

Each of these tools brings me back to what I can control, helping me reset and realign with the version of myself I want to be. Over time, I've found that consistently using these tools helps me not only weather life's storms but also grow stronger and more centered in the process.

There Is No Selfishness in Self-Care

One of the most important lessons I've learned is that taking care of myself is not selfish—it's essential. To truly show up for others, I need to be strong, balanced, and well. Self-care isn't about turning inward and ignoring the world; it's about replenishing my energy so I can give more and love more. By prioritizing my own well-being, I set an example for those around me, inspiring them to do the same.

Self-care creates a ripple effect. When I'm grounded and centered, I'm better equipped to support others. I'm more patient, more compassionate, and more present. And in showing others that self-care is a priority, I encourage them to honor their own well-being too.

Gratitude and Positivity as Fuel

Throughout my journey, I've seen firsthand how gratitude transforms even the hardest moments into opportunities for growth and connection. During my son's health crisis, even before a positive outcome was certain, I cherished the time we had together. This gratitude didn't erase the challenges, but it shifted my focus to the blessings hidden within them.

Earl Nightingale once said, "Learn to enjoy every minute of your life. Be happy now. Don't wait for something outside of yourself to make you happy in the future." These words have guided me through moments of uncertainty, reminding me to find joy and gratitude wherever I can. It's not about avoiding life's challenges but about choosing to be present for ourselves and others, no matter the circumstances.

6

Chapter 6

Nature's Wisdom and the Beauty of Simplicity

In all my years of connecting with nature, one lesson stands out above all the others: nature thrives in its simplicity. It doesn't over complicate or rush. Instead, nature finds balance and flow in its most uncomplicated state. The beauty of nature isn't just in the grand landscapes or endless skies. It's in the way a single leaf dances with the wind, or how water carves its path gently, yet persistently, over time.

Isaac Newton once said, "Nature is pleased with simplicity. And nature is no dummy." There's profound wisdom in that statement. In a world that often encourages us to control, plan, and over analyze, nature reminds us to let go. To trust in the process, even when we can't yet see the details. Simplicity creates space, not for answers to be forced, but for them to arrive in their own perfect timing.

When I embrace simplicity—whether in my thoughts, routines, or surroundings—I open myself to life's natural rhythm. It's in these moments that I feel most aligned, not only with the world around me but with the dreams I hold in my heart. The steps ahead don't have to be clear for me to move forward. Like the seasons, life unfolds in cycles, and I've learned to trust that everything will come into focus when the time is right.

Daydreams and Inspired Action

Daydreaming, like nature's flow, is a practice of simplicity. It allows me to explore endless possibilities without overthinking. Daydreams are not mere fantasies—they are the seeds of inspired action. When I dream about the future, I see more than just goals; I feel the excitement of the life I'm creating.

The beauty of daydreaming is that it doesn't require certainty or a detailed plan. It's about living in the energy of your desires before they manifest, trusting that the how will reveal itself when the timing is right. This openness frees me to dream boldly, without fear of getting it "wrong." When I allow myself to live in the feeling of those dreams—whether it's the joy of future adventures, the satisfaction of meaningful work, or the quiet peace of a life well-lived—I tap into the flow of inspired action.

Some days, the next steps are clear, and I move forward with confidence. Other days, the path feels hazy, and that's okay. When the steps aren't immediately obvious, I trust in the rhythm of life and turn to what I know will always guide me: wellness, simplicity, and nature.

Training for Life: Preparing Without Pressure

I've often said I'm in training for life—not for anything specific, but for whatever comes my way. This perspective has become a cornerstone of how I live. I don't wait for a challenge to focus on health, flexibility, or strength; I build them into my routine now, knowing they'll serve me in ways I may not yet foresee. I see this preparation as a joyful act, not a burden.

I train my body to be strong and active so I can keep up with the grandchildren I don't yet have. I train my mind to be resilient and curious, ready to embrace new opportunities. I train my spirit to stay grounded in gratitude, knowing that life's gifts often come in unexpected forms. This isn't about control—it's about creating a foundation of wellness and openness that allows me to thrive, no matter what the future holds.

I approach this training with a sense of playfulness and curiosity. I move my body because it feels good to feel strong and free, not because of any external demand. I keep my mind engaged through moments of wonder and exploration, knowing that each new experience adds depth to my journey. And I cultivate gratitude in my spirit, grounding myself in the knowledge that life's gifts often arrive unexpectedly.

I'm ready to embrace whatever comes, whether it's running through the grass with future grandchildren or stepping into an exciting new chapter I can't yet imagine. Each day is a chance to tend to myself with care and kindness, building the foundation for a life lived fully and freely.

Trusting in the Process

There's magic in leaving the details to time. Just as nature doesn't force its rhythms, I've learned to trust that the answers I seek will come when I'm ready for them. This trust doesn't mean I sit idly by—it means I focus on what I can do now, knowing that each small action aligns me with my larger journey.

When life feels uncertain, I turn to wellness, simplicity, and nature's rhythm to guide me back to center. They're not just tools; they're a way of life that keeps me aligned with my truest self, ready to thrive in the face of whatever comes next. This mindset frees me to dream without limits, to live in the excitement of what's possible, and to welcome life's unfolding with an open heart.

Living the Dream Now

One of the greatest lessons nature has taught me is that life is not a race to the finish line. The journey—the process of dreaming, growing, and evolving—is where the true magic lies. I've learned not to wait for my dreams to manifest fully before I start enjoying them. Instead, I live in the energy of those dreams now.

Whether it's imagining future connections, adventures, or accomplishments, I allow myself to feel the joy they bring as if they're already here. This doesn't just bring excitement to the present; it aligns me with the future I'm creating. When I step into that energy, I'm not just dreaming—I'm co-creating with life, setting the stage for what's to come.

Nature's Quiet Wisdom

Nature reminds me that nothing beautiful is ever rushed, and nothing worthwhile is ever forced. Its cycles teach me to trust in the flow of life, to be open to change, and to embrace the beauty of the present moment. A single tree doesn't rush to grow—it takes its time, drawing strength from its roots while reaching for the sky. This is how I aim to live: grounded in simplicity, open to possibility, and excited for the future.

By living simply, dreaming boldly, and trusting in the process, I've found a rhythm that feels authentic and fulfilling. The details of how my dreams will unfold are not mine to control, but the energy I bring to each day is. And that energy—grounded in gratitude, joy, and openness—is what will carry me forward, step by step, toward the life I'm meant to live.

7

Chapter 7

The Journey to Conscious Eating

Healthy eating has become more than just a habit—it's a passion, a journey I've embraced both for myself and my family. It's not about perfection but about paying attention, learning, and adjusting to what our bodies need.

Listening to the Body's Signals

One of the biggest lessons I've learned through this journey is the importance of paying attention to how my body reacts to different foods. Certain ingredients—especially processed ones—can cause fatigue, brain fog, or even mood swings, while whole, nutrient-dense foods leave me feeling energized and clear-headed.

This journey isn't about following a strict set of rules but about listening to my body and adjusting accordingly. There are times when my body craves something nourishing and times when it's asking for balance. The key is to honor those signals and trust that my body knows what it needs.

A Family Transformation

This journey hasn't just been mine—it's been a family experience. We've navigated this path together, learning how food affects not only our physical health but also our emotional and mental well-being. Teaching my family about mindful eating has been one of the most rewarding aspects of this journey. It's not just about avoiding harmful ingredients; it's about creating a relationship with food that's healthy, joyful, and sustainable.

Over the years, I've watched my family become more aware of the choices they make. My children know to read labels, to be conscious of what they consume, and to notice how food makes them feel. This awareness is something I hope they carry with them throughout their lives.

In 2014, we made a family commitment to eliminate high fructose corn syrup and hydrogenated oils from our diets. I'll never forget how trans-formative that year was. It wasn't just about what we *took out* of our diet—it was about what we learned and how we felt. Our energy levels improved, our moods stabilized, and we became more mindful about what we put into our bodies. That year taught us so much, not just about food, but about the power of intention and how much control we really have over our health and wellness.

The Journey to Conscious Eating

Healthy eating has been a passion of mine for years, but it wasn't always that way. One of the first books that really changed the way I thought about food was *Fit for Life* by Harvey and Marilyn Diamond. This book taught me something so simple yet incredibly powerful: **listen to your body**. It emphasized the importance of eating in a way that aligns with your body's natural rhythms and needs.

Fit for Life introduced me to the idea of food as fuel, but more importantly, it encouraged me to simplify my approach to eating. Before that, I had been caught up in the complexities of diet trends and trying to follow rigid rules that didn't resonate with how I felt. The book helped me strip all of that away and focus on tuning in to what my body was telling me.

By simplifying my meals—choosing whole, fresh foods and learning to pair them in a way that felt natural—I could finally start to hear the signals my body was sending. I learned how certain foods gave me energy, clarity, and focus, while others left me feeling sluggish or heavy. It wasn't about restriction; it was about **balance and awareness**. That shift in perspective laid the groundwork for everything I would explore in the years to come.

Healthy eating isn't about perfection—it's about finding what works for you and your body, and making adjustments along the way. It's about feeling good, inside and out, and creating a lifestyle that supports your long-term well-being.

Balance is Key

Through all of this, I've learned the importance of balance. It's not about cutting out every indulgence or following a rigid diet—it's about nourishing our bodies while still enjoying life. I've come to a place where I don't restrict myself, but I remain conscious and intentional with my choices. If I've learned anything, it's that our bodies are constantly communicating with us, and the more we pay attention, the better we can care for ourselves.

Nourishing the Brain: The Key to Mental Vitality

I often remind myself:

"How well you nourish your brain determines how well your brain will nurture you."

The relationship between food and mental health is profound. Whole, nutrient-dense foods not only fuel the body but also support brain function, creativity, and emotional balance. When I eat mindfully, my mind feels clearer, my mood brighter, and my ability to face challenges stronger.

When we feed our brains with whole, nutrient-dense foods, we provide the energy it needs to support cognitive function, creativity, and emotional balance. I've found that when I'm mindful of what I eat, not only does my body feel better, but my mind is clearer, my mood is brighter, and I'm able to navigate challenges with greater ease.

But it's not just about food. How we take care of ourselves mentally and emotionally also plays a huge role in brain health. Stress, lack of sleep, and even negative thinking can drain our mental energy, making it harder for the brain to function optimally. By practicing mindfulness, taking time for rest, and being intentional with self-care, we give our brains the space to recharge and thrive.

Brain-Boosting Foods: Coconut Oil and Blueberries

As I've explored how to nourish both my body and mind, I've found that certain foods stand out for their ability to support brain health. Two of my personal favorites are **coconut oil** and **blueberries**—simple, everyday foods that offer profound benefits for mental clarity, focus, and memory.

Coconut Oil: Fuel for the Brain

Coconut oil is often referred to as a super food, and for good reason. It contains medium-chain triglycerides (MCTs), which are easily absorbed by the body and converted into fuel for the brain. MCTs provide a quick, clean source of energy, supporting cognitive function and protecting brain cells from damage. Studies have shown that the fatty acids in coconut oil can improve memory and may even have protective effects against neurodegenerative diseases like Alzheimer's.

For me, incorporating coconut oil into my diet has been an easy and rewarding way to nourish my brain. Whether it's adding a spoonful to my morning coffee or using it in cooking, I've noticed how it supports both my mental clarity and sustained energy throughout the day.

Blueberries: The Brain's Best Friend

Blueberries are another staple in my brain-health toolbox. These little berries are packed with antioxidants, particularly flavonoids, which have been shown to delay brain aging and improve memory. Blueberries help fight oxidative stress and inflammation, both of which can negatively impact brain function over time.

Research shows that regularly eating blueberries may improve communication between brain cells, enhancing cognitive function and helping with memory retention. For me, adding a handful of blueberries to my breakfast or as a snack has become a delicious way to support my mental health and long-term brain function.

Encouragement for Your Journey

Conscious eating begins with curiosity and small steps. Start by listening to your body—how does it feel after certain foods? Begin with a general physical exam, discuss your goals with your physician, and get baseline blood work. If your current practitioner doesn't align with your holistic goals, seek one who does.

This isn't about immediate change or perfection—it's a continual journey of experimentation, learning, and adjusting. Take note of what feels good and what doesn't. Allow your preferences to evolve over time, keeping nutrition and feeling good at the forefront.

Trusting in Simplicity and Balance

Slow down. Listen. Nourish. By grounding yourself in conscious choices, you create a foundation of wellness and vitality that supports you through every chapter of life. The journey to conscious eating isn't a diet or a trend—it's a lifelong relationship with yourself, your health, and the food that fuels your future.

8

Chapter 8

The Pull of Synergy and the Greater Connection

There's a moment when you start to feel the pull of something greater—a force that connects everything in your life. Lately, I've been more aware of that pull, this beautiful sense of **synergy** between people, ideas, and even the natural world. It's as if the universe is aligning things around me, nudging me toward deeper connections, greater collaborations, and a path that feels both expansive and entirely possible.

Synergy is more than just collaboration; it's the realization that we're all part of something bigger than ourselves. When I open myself to this mindset, I see that life isn't about working in isolation or pushing uphill. It's about embracing the natural flow of energy that comes when things—and people—come together in harmony. The opportunities, the insights, the growth—all of it seems to multiply when synergy is at play.

In many ways, this pull I'm feeling is a reminder that we

are never truly alone in our efforts. Everything we do, and everyone we meet, plays a role in our journey. It's as if the universe is quietly orchestrating the perfect people, moments, and challenges to appear in just the right places, pushing us forward even when we don't yet realize it.

I've come to see that this pull toward connection and alignment is a sign to trust the unfolding process. When you recognize the power of synergy, you stop trying to force things to happen and instead start allowing them to happen. It's about stepping into a space where the right people, the right opportunities, and the right energy naturally align, creating something far more powerful than you could have imagined on your own.

The Magic of Synergy in Action

In practical terms, synergy has shown up in all aspects of my life. In my relationships, it's the flow that happens when I'm in sync with those around me—whether it's my family, friends, or colleagues. We bring our individual strengths, ideas, and experiences, but when we work together, it feels like we're creating something greater, something filled with purpose. It's not just about collaborating, it's about combining energies in a way that amplifies everything we're capable of achieving.

The same applies to my creative projects. I've noticed that when I stop trying to control every outcome and instead invite collaboration, inspiration flows effortlessly. It's as if I tap into a greater source of creativity, one that I couldn't access alone. Ideas bloom more fully when shared, and the results often exceed what I envisioned at the start. It's synergy in motion— an unfolding process of creation that's supported by everyone involved.

Synergy and Nature's Reflection

I've also seen synergy reflected in nature, which constantly reminds me of the interconnections of all things. Nature is the perfect example of synergy—everything has its place, its role, and when all parts work together, balance is achieved. The trees, the water, the air, the animals—each one contributes to the harmony of the ecosystem. Nothing stands alone; everything depends on something else to thrive.

This is why I've found so much solace in nature. It's a place where synergy is alive and visible, and where I feel the most connected to that greater energy. Being in nature reminds me that when we align ourselves with the natural flow of life, when we stop resisting or forcing, we begin to thrive in ways we hadn't anticipated.

Practicing Alignment and Believing in Magic

Getting into alignment and recognizing the synergistic moments takes practice and awareness. The more aligned you become and remain, the more magical and long-lasting the moments of heightened synergy become. It's not just about noticing these moments—it's about believing in their power. Don't be afraid to believe in magic. It's not some far-off fantasy; it's woven into the everyday miracles that surround us. Miracles happen every day. Life continues whether you are paying attention or not. But when you choose to show up for yourself—when you align with gratitude, intention, and trust—you invite those miracles into your life.

Gratitude, I've learned, is one of the most powerful tools for aligning with synergy. I am certain it all grows like compound interest. The more gratitude I feel, the more I see to be grateful for, and so on. Gratitude opens the door to noticing the magic already present in your life, and that awareness is what creates space for even more.

The Path Forward

The pull of synergy is a reminder that you're part of something greater than yourself. It asks you to trust in the flow of life, to believe in the magic of connection, and to allow yourself to show up fully for the journey. Start with gratitude. Start with showing up for yourself. And watch as the universe begins to align things in ways you never thought possible. Each step forward becomes not just a move toward your goals, but a part of something bigger, something filled with magic, purpose, and endless possibility.

Daily Intentions: A Practice for Everyone

Some call it prayer.

Some call it meditation.

Some say affirmations.

Others call it setting intentions or reflection.

Whatever name resonates with you, the act itself is what matters. It's not about the label or how you do it—it's about creating the space, finding the time, and allowing yourself to connect with what you truly want for your life.

Start with the broad strokes: **Health. Wellness. Peace.** These foundational intentions anchor you in the energy you want to carry throughout your day. They don't require elaborate rituals—just a moment of stillness, a breath, and a focus on what feels right.

As life ebbs and flows, allow yourself to add detail. Maybe you're visualizing healing, clarity, or strength. Maybe you're calling in abundance, joy, or resolution to a specific challenge.

There's no right or wrong way—only your way.

Find what works for you, and make it a daily practice. Whether it's in the morning light, during a quiet walk, or as you lay your head down at night, take that time to reflect, align, and set your intentions. The ripple effects can be profound, shaping not only your day but the trajectory of your life.

Find the time. Find the space.

And show up for yourself.

9

Chapter 9

Embracing Life's Lessons and the Power of Connection

As I reflect on the journey of alignment, I realize that life's most profound lessons often emerge from our relationships and challenges. The people we love, the hardships we endure, and the moments that redefine us are all part of the universe's way of guiding us back to ourselves. These experiences, whether they bring joy or sorrow, teach us resilience, compassion, and the beauty of connection.

Losing my father and later my mother were defining moments that forever altered my understanding of love, loss, and legacy. They were my first teachers, each imparting wisdom that continues to shape me. My father taught me the power of presence, the quiet strength of kindness, and the importance of integrity. My mother had a presence that was both gentle and complex. To the outside world, she seemed quiet, almost reserved, yet to those of us close to her, she was anything but silent. She had a way of retreating into herself, reflecting on life in a way that sometimes felt distant, yet it was her own way of processing the world. Her support wasn't always obvious or traditional, and it took time for me to see how deeply it ran beneath the surface. Now, I understand her in ways I couldn't before, and I love and miss her with a depth that only comes from recognizing the intricate beauty of who she truly was. Their absence left a void, but also a lasting imprint, guiding me even now.

Life brought other unexpected changes as well. Losing my long-standing job was one such turning point—forcing me to step out of my comfort zone and redefine what success means. And then, watching my son Matthew undergo an organ transplant was perhaps the most challenging journey of all, one that taught me about courage, hope, and the strength we find in love and family. Through his journey, I discovered a well of resilience within myself I didn't know existed.

Starting a new job, venturing into writing this book, and reflecting on other influential people and moments along the way—each experience has added a layer of growth, helping me to see life as an ever-evolving canvas of lessons and transformations. Together, these stories form the fabric of who I am, revealing the power of alignment, not just with the universe, but with the values and connections that matter most.

In the following chapters, I'll share these stories with you. Not just as memories, but as pieces of a larger puzzle, each one offering its own insight, challenge, and gift. Through them, I hope to convey that even in the face of loss, change, and uncertainty, there is always something beautiful waiting to unfold. Life, in all its complexity, continues to lead us toward the fullest expression of who we are meant to be.

Lessons from My Parents: Strength and Acceptance

My father embodied strength—not just physical resilience, but a quiet, steadfast strength that came from deep within. He showed me that true strength isn't loud or forceful; it's a steady presence that can endure life's storms with grace. His strength was in the way he faced challenges and how he showed up for his family, teaching me the power of being grounded and dependable.

The Gentle Giant: My Father's Quiet Strength

My father, often referred to by my mother as the "Gentle Giant," was a man of quiet but profound strength. Diagnosed with acromegaly as a young man, his life was shaped by challenges that would have overwhelmed most. At 18, he underwent surgery that doctors believed would limit his life expectancy to his 40s and prevent him from having children. Yet, he defied those expectations, living until the age of 59 and raising three children along the way. He even managed to fit in 10 years of hard earned retirement. His life was a testament to resilience, determination, and an unwavering sense of purpose.

He approached life with a remarkable down-to-earth nature, valuing common sense and simplicity. While others might have been consumed by fear or regret given his diagnosis and prognosis, my father instead embraced what was. He lived fully, showing us what it meant to face life's uncertainties with courage and grace.

On his 59th birthday, my father was diagnosed with terminal cancer. This was a cruel twist of fate, as though life were reminding us that no one is promised forever. Yet, his response was nothing short of extraordinary. Rather than dwelling on the tragedy of it all, he accepted it with a quiet strength that amazed everyone around him. His focus turned immediately to those he was leaving behind—my mother, his children, and the life he had built with so much care.

He spent his final days setting my mother up for success, organizing what he could to ensure she would thrive without him. His concern for us was evident in every decision he made. He did his best to shield his children from the worst of his battle, not wanting us to carry the burden of his pain. His strength during this time wasn't just physical or emotional—it was deeply spiritual, rooted in a profound acceptance of life as it was.

One of the most profound lessons my father taught me was about acceptance. Watching him navigate his final journey was like witnessing a master class in grace. He never complained, never railed against the unfairness of it all. Instead, he showed us that there is a certain peace that comes from embracing what cannot be changed. This lesson has stayed with me, shaping how I approach challenges in my own life.

Despite the heartache of losing him, I am comforted by the life he lived and the legacy he left. He was a protector, a provider, and a teacher. His quiet strength spoke louder than any words ever could. He showed me that true strength is not in resisting life's challenges but in accepting them with grace and dignity.

Even in his absence, my father's influence continues to guide me. His love for life, his acceptance of what was, and his devotion to his family are gifts that I carry with me every day. I see his strength in myself, in my siblings, and in the quiet moments when I reflect on the profound lessons he left behind.

My father may not have lived to see his 60th birthday, but

his spirit remains timeless. He was, and always will be, our "Gentle Giant," a man who walked through life with uncommon grace, teaching us that strength isn't always loud—it can be quiet, steady, and unshakable.

My Unique Mother: My biggest Fan

My mother was a quiet source of strength and compassion, and I had the privilege of watching her evolve over the years. There were moments when I saw glimpses of her growth, subtle transformations that deepened her kindness and self-awareness. Yet, despite her inner strength and her gift for loving others, I don't believe she ever fully bloomed into the person she could have become. It was as though there were parts of her that remained hidden, dreams and possibilities she hadn't had the chance to explore.

This sense of her journey being unfinished added a bittersweet note to my understanding of her. She gave to those around her, sometimes at the expense of her own desires. In witnessing her story, I learned that while loving and supporting others is beautiful, it's also vital to nurture our own growth, to give ourselves permission to expand and to chase our own aspirations.

My mother taught me the importance of compassion and acceptance, and she showed me that growth is possible even when life doesn't allow us to fully bloom. Her legacy is a reminder to me that while life's demands are often great, we owe it to ourselves to pursue our own paths. In honoring her journey, I feel a renewed commitment to mine, knowing that she'd want me to fully embrace who I am meant to become.

10

Chapter 10

My Mother - My biggest fan

Don't Grow Up So Fast

One of my earliest memories of my mother is her holding me close and softly saying, "Don't grow up so fast." I was the youngest by five years, always trying to keep up with my siblings, eager to be older, to do what they did. But she saw something in me that I couldn't yet see in myself—a sweetness, an innocence she wanted to protect, a fleeting childhood she knew would pass too quickly.

In her gentle plea, I can feel her love, her longing to hold on to the moments when I was still her little one. There was a vulnerability there, a quiet desire to keep me close, just as I was. Even now, I can almost feel her arms around me, that simple moment when time seemed to pause, and all that mattered was being held and loved.

I reflect on this memory often, especially now. At the time, I didn't fully understand her words. I was too focused on growing up, on catching up. But looking back, I can see her tenderness, her wish to slow time, to cherish the days when I was small and still within her reach. She wanted to keep me little, not because she feared change, but because she knew how precious those moments were, how quickly they would slip away.

This memory is a reminder of the love that never left, even as I grew and found my own way. She held on to that image of me, her youngest, her little one, with all the love and care that she quietly carried. And in the end, that love is something I carry too—a gift she gave me in those simple words, "Don't grow up so fast."

A New Freedom

After my father passed, a quiet shift began to unfold within my mother. It was as though she had been given permission—not by anyone else, but by life itself—to step into a fuller version of herself. I don't know if it was something any of us noticed immediately, but over time, I began to see a new strength emerge in her, a resilience that hadn't been as visible before. It was as if, in losing her role as a wife, she found a space where she could simply be herself.

My father was never restrictive, yet there was a freedom she discovered in his absence that was hers alone. She began to embrace her individuality more openly, finding her way as a person defined not by someone else, but by her own essence. I didn't always understand it then, but now I see that it was a moment of transformation. She was learning how to exist on her own terms, no longer just somebody's wife, but her own unique person.

This transformation wasn't loud or obvious; it was quiet, like so much of who she was. She grew into herself subtly, one day at a time, and I could see it in the small things—the confidence in her choices, the steadiness in her gaze, and a new lightness that had room to shine. It was as though she had found a strength she hadn't needed to show before, a strength that became her quiet companion.

Reflecting back, I realize that this was a pivotal time for both of us. I was beginning my own journey of self-discovery, and while I thought I was there to support her, she was also quietly showing me how to embrace change, how to grow into oneself with grace. Watching her find herself after such a profound loss was a lesson in resilience, a reminder that even in the hardest moments, there's room for renewal, for becoming something more.

A Quiet Weekend in Oswego

My mother and I took one weekend trip together. The weekend in Oswego was a rare pause, a quiet interlude in the midst of my father's illness. It was just the two of us—my mother and me—spending time together in a way we rarely had the chance to do. We found ourselves by the pool, her with a puzzle book in hand, me with a novel. There was no pressure to talk, no need to fill the silence. We simply existed side by side, each lost in our own worlds, yet deeply present with each other.

I can still feel the warmth of the sun, the quiet sounds around us, the soft rustle of pages and pencil strokes as we settled into that simple rhythm. That weekend, I saw her in a different light. There was a calm, a sense of ease that I hadn't always recognized in her. She wasn't one for big trips or grand gestures, and her love often showed itself in understated ways. But that weekend, in the silence by the pool, I felt the depth of her love—a love that didn't need words or explanations.

It was the only trip we ever took together, just the two of us. And maybe that's why it holds such a cherished place in my heart. In that quiet space, I caught a glimpse of her as she was: unique, a bit mysterious, and wholly herself. It's a memory I return to often, especially now, as it captures her essence in a way that words never could.

Seeing Care in Calmness and Unpredictable Grace

As a child and young adult, I often found my mother both intriguing and a little baffling. She wasn't always quiet or reserved. She had her own ways of showing up—moments when her unique eccentricity would come to the surface, sometimes surprising us, sometimes even embarrassing us. But that unpredictability, those flashes of her uninhibited spirit, were simply part of her charm. To me, she was beautifully unique, someone who embraced her individuality without asking for approval or fearing judgment.

It took time and maturity to see her fully, to appreciate the complex layers that made her who she was. Growing up, I sometimes questioned whether her calm, untroubled nature was a lack of concern. Once, I even asked her about it. She simply told me, "I don't worry. If something were wrong with you, I'd feel it." At the time, I couldn't grasp the depth of those words. It wasn't until later, when I had enough life behind me, that I started to understand.

Her care wasn't in worrying over the little things—it was in trusting that she would know, instinctively, if something was truly amiss. She seemed to live by an inner compass that guided her without the need for constant explanations or reassurances. As I grew, she watched my journey and often told me she admired my strength and growth. But what I've come to realize is that much of that strength came from her influence, from witnessing her quiet yet unapologetic way of being, from seeing how she navigated life on her own terms.

Her presence taught me that real strength isn't always loud or conventional. It can be quirky, unstructured, and unpredictable, showing up when we least expect it. She left me with a deeper understanding that love, care, and resilience come in countless forms—some loud and visible, others quietly woven into the fabric of everyday life.

My Unique Mother

My mother had a quiet, unique beauty that wasn't defined by others' acceptance or judgment. She simply was. She had an eccentricity, a quiet quirkiness that made her different, but she never seemed too bothered by whether people accepted her or not. She lived in her own way, neither seeking approval nor making apologies for who she was. Her uniqueness wasn't something she flaunted or hid out of shame—it was just a part of her. She moved through life with a quiet strength, never making a big deal out of the fact that she didn't always fit in. In a world that often demands conformity, she just existed on her own terms, without the need to explain herself.

She wasn't always accepted by the world around her, but that didn't seem to bother her. She just kept being herself, unshaken by the judgments or misunderstandings of others. And while she may not have let her full light shine for the world to see, I saw it. I saw her beauty in the little things—her humor, her quirks, her quiet ways of seeing the world. That's the part of her I carry with me, and it's what makes her memory so vibrant in my heart.

Losing a mother, especially one who held such a profound place in your heart, leaves a space that nothing else quite fills. It's as if she's still with you in those cherished memories, in every gentle reminder of her love, yet the ache of missing her remains.

A New Kind of Connection

When my mother passed, it was a complete surprise. There was no warning, no time to prepare, and yet she left this world so peacefully. It felt as though she simply slipped away, carrying with her the same quiet grace she had brought to many moments in life. The shock of her passing was immense, but what followed was something I never expected.

In the months leading up to her passing, I had felt a new closeness with her—something deep and trans-formative. It was as if we were standing on the edge of the best relationship we'd ever had, ready to step into it together. When she left, I thought that connection might disappear with her physical body. But something amazing happened.

That feeling of closeness didn't leave me. Instead, it grew in a way I never could have imagined. I feel her presence every day. It's as though she's guiding me—not in the same way she did when she was here, but in a different and profoundly meaningful way. Perhaps she had always been guiding me this way, and now I simply feel it more clearly.

Her passing, though sudden, brought a profound realization: the bonds we share with those we love are not limited to the physical world. While I miss her human presence deeply, I am comforted knowing that our connection has only transformed, not ended. Her influence is now woven into my journey, and I carry it with me in ways that bring peace, strength, and a sense of purpose.

Chapter 11

The Power of Expectations: The Pygmalion Effect

There's a subtle, powerful force that we often overlook in our daily lives—the effect that our expectations have on the people around us and on ourselves. It's called the **Pygmalion Effect**, and it suggests that when we believe in someone's potential, we can actually influence them to rise to that level of belief.

I've seen this play out in my own life, both in subtle ways and in more profound moments. We're constantly shaping and being shaped by the expectations we place on ourselves and others. When someone truly believes in you—when they see something special, something capable in you—it lights a fire. You begin to perform, to grow, to meet that belief with action, even when you didn't know you had it in you.

It's the same when I've believed in others, especially in moments when they've doubted themselves. I've seen how a small shift in my perspective, a raised expectation, can unlock something within them. It's a ripple effect. What we expect, we often create.

But what's even more powerful is when we turn this effect inward—when we start to believe in our own potential. The way we speak to ourselves, the expectations we set for what we are capable of, can be the difference between staying stuck and stepping into the life we want. **Self-fulfilling prophecies** aren't just myths—they're at the heart of how we grow. The more we trust in our abilities, the more we start to see opportunities that align with that trust.

I've had to learn to shift my own expectations about what's possible, not just for myself but for the people I love and work with. When you raise your expectations, you create space for something greater to emerge. It's not just about hoping for the best—it's about truly believing in the potential that's already there.

The Role of Mindset

What's most fascinating about the Pygmalion Effect is that it's rooted in mindset. It's about the quiet, subconscious ways we influence the world around us. We may not even realize how powerful our beliefs are, but they shape our actions, our words, and how we respond to others.

The lesson here is simple: **Expect better.** Not just in a demanding way, but in a loving, supportive way. Expect that growth is possible. Expect that even in the hardest of times, there is potential for transformation. Believe in the strength of those around you, and most importantly, believe in yourself.

In this journey, I've come to understand that what we expect, we receive. And as I continue to challenge my own expectations and set higher ones for myself and others, I've watched the world shift in response.

The Power of Expectations in Raising Our Children

As parents, we often don't realize just how much our expectations shape the lives of our children. When Matthew was born, Robert and I were young—full of love but not entirely prepared for the incredible journey of parenthood. Like many young parents, we learned through trial and error. There were struggles, as we tried to balance our youth, our inexperience, and the weight of being responsible for this new life. Looking back, I can see that we were learning as we went, and Matthew grew up with us as much as we grew as parents.

But what I didn't see back then was *how* much Matthew was teaching *us*. His resilience, his curiosity, and even his challenges became our greatest lessons. We may have been his parents, but in many ways, Matthew was guiding us—showing us how to be more patient, how to nurture, and how to believe in ourselves as much as we believed in him. He taught us that parenthood is less about having all the answers and more about growing through the experience, side by side.

As I began exploring ideas like the Pygmalion Effect, I started to understand just how much our expectations influence the way children grow. It wasn't just about what we expected from Matthew—it was about what *he* expected from us, and how his trust in us pushed us to become better, more thoughtful parents.

By the time Michael and Robbie were born—over 10 years later—everything felt different. Along with our experience with Matthew, I had already begun diving deeply into concepts like the **Pygmalion Effect**. The loss of my father a few years prior sparked a time of great change for me personally, and I was reflecting deeply on life, legacy, and the impact we have on others. It's during this period that I realized how much our beliefs and expectations shape not just ourselves, but the people we love most—our children. I realized that by believing in their potential, we were giving them the space to become their best selves.

With Michael and Robbie, I began to intentionally apply what I was learning. I understood that if I could believe in their potential, they would naturally rise to meet those beliefs. I wasn't just setting expectations for their behavior or achievements—I was setting expectations for the kind of people they could become. I believed they could grow into compassionate, kind, and resilient individuals, and because I held that belief, I started to see them become exactly that.

The Shift in Parenting: Believing in Potential

Matthew's early years were different, and not just because we were young. At that point, I hadn't fully grasped the power of expectations. We were just trying to get through the days, often overwhelmed by the demands of life. But when I started applying what I had learned from concepts like the Pygmalion Effect, I realized that by shifting my mindset, I could help shift my children's futures.

With Michael and Robbie, there was a distinct difference in how we raised them. I wasn't just reacting to their behaviors or correcting them—I was setting the bar for how I wanted them to see themselves. I believed in their ability to grow, to learn from mistakes, to be kind, and to persevere. And they met those expectations because they felt that belief from me and Robert.

With Matthew, we had learned along the way. By the time he was seven, we were growing into more conscious parents. And I think that's one of the great lessons we take with us:

the realization that we're always learning, always evolving, and that's okay. The Pygmalion Effect isn't just about how we influence others—it's about how we grow alongside them, raising our own expectations for who we can be as parents, as partners, and as individuals.

Learning from Experience and Growth

What made a difference for our family wasn't just what we expected from our children—it was the love and faith we wrapped around those expectations. We believed in their potential without putting pressure on them to be perfect. We expected growth, not perfection. We encouraged learning from mistakes, not avoiding them. And as we learned to raise our own expectations for ourselves as parents, our children rose to meet the positive expectations we held for them.

That's the power of the Pygmalion Effect—what we believe matters. Not just for ourselves, but for those we love most. And as we grew in understanding, we became better parents for Matthew, Michael, and Robbie. Looking back, I see the difference in how we raised them, and I am grateful for the lessons we learned along the way.

A Shift in Parenting

By the time Michael and Robbie came into the picture, Robert and I had grown, both as individuals and as parents. We weren't just reacting to situations anymore; we were more intentional, more thoughtful about how we wanted to shape our children's lives. The lessons we learned with Matthew allowed us to take a more balanced approach with his brothers.

With Michael and Robbie, I began to apply what I had learned more consciously. I understood the power of believing in their potential, and I made a point to set expectations that were high but loving. It wasn't about perfection; it was about growth. I wanted them to know that they could make mistakes, learn from them, and keep moving forward with confidence.

This approach became particularly evident during their toddler years. Trips to the grocery store or other errands transformed from anxiety-filled tasks into well-behaved adventures. Rather than feeling overwhelmed by the chaos that often accompanies toddlers in public, I found myself enjoying these outings, marveling at their ability to rise to the occasion. It wasn't about expecting flawless behavior—it was about setting a tone of calm and mutual respect, which they seemed to reflect back.

That belief in their abilities wasn't something I had fully grasped when Matthew was young, but by the time Michael and Robbie were born, I had come to see how powerful it could be. The more we believed in their abilities, the more they rose to meet those expectations, proving again and again that our faith in them was well-placed.

The Journey of Growth

The Pygmalion Effect became a part of our parenting, but more than that, it became a part of our family's journey of growth. Matthew had laid the foundation, teaching us the importance of patience, trust, and love. He helped us become the parents we needed to be for his younger brothers, and for that, I am deeply grateful.

Parenting isn't a one-way street. Our children teach us just as much—if not more—than we teach them. With Matthew, we learned to adapt, to grow, to have faith in ourselves and in him. With Michael and Robbie, we applied those lessons in a more intentional way, setting expectations not just for them, but for ourselves as parents. We learned to believe in the possibility of growth, to expect progress over perfection, and to create a space where our children could thrive.

In the end, the power of expectations—the Pygmalion Effect—wasn't just about shaping our children's futures. It was about shaping our own. And as we raised our children, we found that we were raising ourselves, too—becoming the people and the parents we were meant to be.

The Promise to Lift the Bar

The journey of parenting, of growth, and of believing in potential is one that never truly ends. As I reflect on the lessons we've learned, the challenges we've overcome, and the victories we've celebrated, I realize how much of this journey is about continually raising the bar—not just for our children, but for ourselves.

It's a promise I make to my family, to myself, and to everyone whose life I have the privilege of touching: to always see the best in others, to set expectations that inspire growth, and to nurture an environment where those around me feel supported and encouraged to rise to their full potential.

This isn't about perfection—it never was. It's about believing in the beauty of progress, the power of trying again, and the incredible strength that comes from being surrounded by love and faith. By lifting the bar for ourselves and others, we create a ripple effect that carries far beyond what we can see.

And so, I end this chapter with a promise: to keep believing, to keep growing, and to keep creating space for greatness to unfold—not just in my family, but in every connection I'm fortunate enough to make. I invite you to do the same, to lift the bar for yourself and those you love, and to watch as the magic of expectations transforms your world.

12

Chapter 12

A Spark of Curiosity

In 2012, the world seemed caught up in the conversation about the end of the Mayan calendar. It wasn't a fear-driven panic that gripped me, but rather a deep sense of curiosity. What if this wasn't the end, but a shift—a transition into something new, a different way of living or seeing the world? The idea stirred something deep inside me, a spark of curiosity that I couldn't ignore.

This spark didn't appear out of nowhere. Years earlier, I had stumbled across Napoleon Hill's *The Secret of Success in 16 Lessons* at a church garage sale. It wasn't just an ordinary find; it was a discovery that shifted my perspective entirely. As I read those books, I felt as if someone had handed me a blueprint—not just for success, but for living with intention.

Hill's lessons were trans-formative in their simplicity and profound in their truth. They weren't just about achieving outward goals; they were about aligning your thoughts, emotions, and actions with a deeper sense of purpose. The books encouraged patience, resilience, and trust in the process of growth. I wasn't looking for instant results, and I didn't expect overnight success. Instead, I embraced the idea of planting seeds and tending to them over time, trusting that the harvest would come when the time was right.

By the time 2012 arrived, I realized that the changes happening around me were also happening within me. I was letting go of fear and uncertainty, replacing them with curiosity and quiet determination. I no longer needed to control every outcome. Instead, I began to trust in the universal laws I had been exploring—particularly the Law of Attraction.

That same year, I made a significant shift in my own life. I left a job of 16 years—a job that had brought stability but no longer felt aligned with my growth. I had manifested a new position, one that was within walking distance from my home. While this new job didn't resonate as a perfect fit, it served a critical purpose: it gave me the space and perspective to apply the lessons I had been learning. It was a proving ground for my growing understanding of the universal laws, especially the importance of focusing on what you want, not on what you fear.

The time away from my original job was trans-formative. It allowed me to see myself with fresh eyes. I grew taller—not in the physical sense, but in my confidence, my self-awareness, and my ability to trust in the path I was on. When I eventually returned to my old workplace, I wasn't the same person who had left. My growth was undeniable, and it was noticed. The foundation I had been building through curiosity, patience, and intentional living was beginning to bear fruit.

During this period of transition, my family and I made changes that further supported our growth. We began to enhance our eating habits, diving deeper into the idea that food isn't just fuel—it's a way to nurture the body and mind. Exercise evolved, too, becoming less of a chore and more of an exploration. We approached it with the same curiosity that had guided so many of our choices. Whether it was trying new activities or learning more about how our bodies worked, the journey was one of discovery rather than obligation.

Looking back, the shift I experienced during those years was subtle but profound. It wasn't marked by dramatic moments or sweeping changes. Instead, it was a steady unfolding—a quiet revolution that touched every aspect of my life. The decision to leave my job, the lessons from Napoleon Hill, the growing awareness of how universal laws shaped my reality—all of it came together to create a period of growth that felt both magical and inevitable.

The beauty of this journey was that it didn't require me to have all the answers. I didn't need to know exactly where I was headed or how I would get there. All I needed was the willingness to stay curious, to keep learning, and to trust the process.

The Mayan calendar didn't mark the end of the world. For me, it marked a new beginning—a time of awakening, exploration, and quiet confidence. It was a reminder that life is always in motion, always inviting us to grow, to learn, and to align ourselves with the possibilities that await.

The seeds I planted during those years—through curiosity, through intentional choices, through the willingness to step out of my comfort zone—continue to grow. They've shaped who I am today and remind me that every transition, no matter how uncertain it may seem, holds the potential for transformation.

13

Chapter 13

A Life Unfolding

Matthew's Journey and the Synchronicity of Loss and Healing

Life has a way of unfolding in unexpected, yet profoundly meaningful ways. It doesn't always make sense in the moment, but when we look back, we often see a kind of divine timing, a synchronicity that ties together the moments of our greatest challenges with our deepest growth. This is the story of how my life, and my son Matthew's journey, unfolded in such a way that left me awestruck by the way loss, healing, and transformation intertwined to create a narrative I never could have imagined.

The Job Loss: A Moment of Trust and Reconnection

After 26 years at my job, the sudden loss was a shock. At first, I felt disoriented and unsure of what the future would hold. But something remarkable happened within just a few days—I realized that the timing, while unexpected, was exactly what I needed. Deep down, I knew it was **time**. It was as if the universe had been working behind the scenes, nudging me toward this moment. I had been longing for freedom, for time to reconnect with myself, and suddenly, that freedom was right in front of me.

Rather than feeling lost, I felt an overwhelming sense of **trust**—a deep, unshakable belief that the universe was working with me, not against me. I embraced this newfound time as an opportunity to reconnect with who I was outside of the routine and structure of my career. For the first time in decades, I wasn't defined by deadlines, meetings, or responsibilities. I was free to explore myself in ways I hadn't been able to in years.

That first month was a gift. I spent my days reflecting, rediscovering old passions, and giving myself permission to simply **be**. I had longed for this kind of space for so long, and now it was mine. I didn't know what would come next, but I didn't need to. I had a deep sense of knowing that everything would unfold exactly as it was meant to.

And then, Matthew's diagnosis came.

Suddenly, I understood the timing even more clearly. The universe had cleared my path so that I could fully devote myself to what mattered most: my son. The job loss, which could have felt devastating, became a blessing—a moment of realignment that allowed me to be present for Matthew's journey in a way that would have been impossible otherwise. It was as if the universe had cleared space in my life, making room for me to be fully present during the most critical time for my family.

Matthew's Transplant Journey: A Miracle in the Midst of Loss

When we learned that Matthew needed a liver transplant, our world shifted once again. It was a moment filled with fear and uncertainty, but somehow, through it all, we believed—deeply, unwaveringly—that a good outcome was possible. The call we had been waiting for finally came: a liver had become available. In the moment of receiving that call, our hearts were filled with hope, but I also couldn't escape the awareness of what that call meant for another family.

For one family, this was a moment of unimaginable grief—the loss of a life. While we were living our miracle, another family was living their darkest hour. The polarity of joy and sorrow hit me in a way I had never experienced before. I knew that Matthew's second chance at life came from the loss of someone else's, and that duality was not lost on me. It deepened my gratitude, made every moment we spent in the hospital together feel even more precious.

During those long days at Matthew's bedside, I felt an overwhelming sense of appreciation for the time I was given to be with him. Freed from the pressures of my job, I could be fully present in a way I had never been able to before.

Finding Balance Through the Law of Polarity

Through this experience, I came to understand the **Law of Polarity** in a way I never had before. The duality of life—joy and sorrow, loss and gain—became more real to me than ever. It wasn't just a philosophical concept; it was my lived reality. The fear of losing Matthew existed alongside the joy of spending time with him, and both emotions fed into each other. The sorrow of knowing another family had lost their loved one deepened my gratitude for the gift of life that had been given to mine. The loss of my job, which at first felt like a devastating blow, became a blessing that gave me the time and space to focus on what truly mattered.

In embracing both sides of these experiences, I found a sense of balance. Life is not always about choosing joy over sorrow, but about **embracing both**—allowing them to coexist and understanding that one often gives meaning to the other. Without the fear of losing Matthew, I may not have been able to fully appreciate the time I had with him during his recovery. Without the loss of my job, I would not have had the freedom to be there for him in the way that I was. Without the sorrow of one family's loss, we would not have experienced the miracle of Matthew's transplant.

A Life Forever Changed

This journey was, without a doubt, a life-changing experience—not just for Matthew, but for me as well. It changed the way I see the world, the way I approach challenges, and the way I understand the interconnections of joy and sorrow. I learned that the things we think of as losses are often part of a larger plan, one that we may not fully understand until much later. My life, which felt so derailed when I lost my job, unfolded into something far more meaningful than I could have imagined.

Now, I can look back and see the beauty in how everything came together—the synchronicity of events that led to Matthew's healing and my own growth. It was, and continues to be, a reminder that even in our darkest moments, there is a greater story being written—one that we are often too close to see, but that, when revealed, shows us the beauty of life's unfolding.

14

Chapter 14

Conclusion: A Life in Harmony

As I sit here reflecting on the pages of this book, I see a snapshot of where I am in my life right now—a beautiful, ever-evolving journey of learning, growing, and trusting. This book is not an ending; it's simply a pause, a moment to share the magic of the Universal Laws as I've come to know them and to encourage others to explore their own paths.

The more I trust in the Universal Laws, the more aligned I feel, and the more effortlessly life seems to unfold. I no longer feel the need to force outcomes or control every step. Instead, I ebb and flow with life, letting it guide me where I need to be. In this space of trust, I've found peace, strength, and an unshakable belief that everything is always working out for me—no matter how winding the path may seem.

To you, the reader, I offer this encouragement:

Study these laws. Look for the lessons life is always offering you. Have fun with it. There is no rush to "figure it all out" or reach some distant finish line. Life is not about arriving—it's about unfolding. Plant the seeds of your dreams with intention, nurture them with love and patience, and watch as they grow in ways you never could have imagined.

Trust the Process

Use intention to guide your thoughts and actions. Ask yourself:

- Who do I want to be?
- What life do I want to live?

Be intentional with your answers. Your dreams have power, and so do your thoughts. Align them with gratitude, kindness, and love, and watch the energy around you begin to shift.

Small Steps, Lifelong Growth

- **Practice Gratitude**: It is the foundation for shifting energy and creating abundance. The more you look for the good, the more you will find.
- **Change Your Perspective**: When challenges arise, ask yourself, "What lesson is here for me?" Sometimes a simple shift in perspective opens the door to unexpected blessings. Even in the hardest times, there is often something to be grateful for. Looking for the gratitude is an easy way to change perspective.
- **Self-Care Is Not Selfish**: You must be strong to care for others. Lead by example—show your loved ones what it

looks like to prioritize well-being, balance, and joy.

- **Keep It Simple**: Growth doesn't need to be complicated. Start small. Build over time. Allow your dreams and intentions to evolve as the time feels right.
- **Give Yourself Grace**: This is *your* journey. Fill it with self-compassion and understanding. Be patient with yourself, celebrate the wins, and trust that every step counts.

For Those Who Have Experienced the Magic

If you have felt the power of the Universal Laws, keep going. Keep nurturing your curiosity, exploring new ways to align with life's flow, and pushing those ripples of positivity forward. Life will still knock us down—it's inevitable—but the real magic lies in how quickly we find our way back up. When we encourage each other to rise, to trust, and to grow, the ripple effect becomes unstoppable.

Let's continue to inspire and uplift one another. Let's share what we've learned, encourage others to explore these truths, and keep that energy moving forward. You never know how far one simple act of positivity can travel or how deeply it might change someone's life.

Your Journey, Your Light

This is your journey—one that no one else can walk for you. Fill it with love, compassion, and an unshakable belief in yourself. There's no race to the finish line, no "right" way to do it. Be curious. Be kind. Trust the process, and embrace the beauty of life unfolding just as it's meant to.

A Final Note

As I close this book, I feel immense gratitude—for the lessons I've learned, for the Universal Laws that continue to guide me, for the curiosity that leads me, and for the magic of life unfolding one moment at a time. I hope this book inspires you to trust in your own journey, to look for alignment in all things, and to embrace the process of becoming.

If you've felt this magic, let's keep it going. Let's push those ripples far and wide, encouraging as many as we can to find their light, rise after every fall, and live fully.

Life is beautiful when you let it flow. Keep dreaming. Keep growing. Keep believing. The best is yet to come.

With love, light, and trust in the journey,

Cynthia ❤